SERVICES

Worship Feast

50 Complete Multisensory Services for Youth

WORSHIP FEAST:

50 Complete Multisensory Services for Youth

This book is printed on acid-free, recycled paper.

ISBN 0-687-06357-4

At the time of publication, all websites were correct and operational.

MANUFACTURED IN THE UNITED STATES OF AMERICA

03 04 05 06 07 08 09 10 11 12—10 9 8 7 6 5 4 3 2 1

SERVICES

Worship Feast

50 Complete Multisensory Services for Youth

Abingdon Press
Nashville

Meet the Writers

Reverend Daniel S. White is pastor of worship and worship team coordinator at Christ Church of Oak Brook, in suburban Chicago. He coordinates musicians, pastors, and technology staff so that Christ Church might experience God-exalting, people-engaging worship. He leads the worship staff in producing six worship services in three distinct expressions of worship (traditional/ Reformed, praise/contemporary, ancient-future/contemplative). He is the pastor for Sojourn, a missional community engaging in multisensory worship experiences. During his years as a youth pastor, he discovered a passion for communicating the gospel in authentic and engaging ways. He lives in Oak Brook with his wife, Lisha, and daughters, Sophie and Chloe.

Tim Gossett is the director of Christian education and Youth Ministries at Collegiate United Methodist Church and Wesley Foundation, in Ames, Iowa. He is passionate about connecting current technology to the ancient practice of Christian worship.

Beth Miller is director of youth ministries at First United Methodist Church, in Ann Arbor, Michigan, and is the writer and director for The Strangely Warmed Players drama troupe. She is excited about helping youth actively experience worship through the creative arts.

Jonathon Norman is a United Methodist youth pastor in Nashville, Tennessee. He has participated in worship retreats and has a special interest in the needs and passions of postmodern young people. He writes poetry and song. Jonathon is a native of Nashville where he lives with his wife and son.

Jennifer A. Youngman is a development editor of youth resources for The United Methodist Publishing House. She recently spent a week at the Taizé community in France, singing, praying, meditating, and worshiping. She is passionate about creating space for young people to experience God in worship. Jenny lives in Nashville with her husband, Mark, and dogs Roxanne and Wrigley Field.

"Taste and see that the LORD is good" Psalm 34:8.

Worship Is a Feast for the Senses . . . .

Contents

"Taste and see that the LORD is good" Psalm 34:8.

Worship Is a Feast for the Senses. . . .

"Taste and see that the LORD is good" Psalm 34:8.

Worship Is a Feast for the Senses. . .

Worship at Sojourn

A Postmodern Sojourn

One model of experiential worship comes from a ministry in which I participate called Sojourn. This ministry is a bit of a theological stew of Orthodox symbolism, charismatic freedom, seeker-sensitivity, and a Reformed view of the proclamation event. We are unapologetic about being an expression of spirituality that is distinctly Christian. Many expressions of spirituality abound these days and faith is a hot topic. So we simply gather together and say "This is how our specific community in a specific context does the Christianity thing." Our approach is not merely an attempt to be edgy, just authentic.

What normally comes to mind when I think of worship is singing. I have been trained to think so. But worship is so much more; in fact, everything a follower of Jesus does is supposed to be worship. At Sojourn, when we gather for worship, we do a lot more than sing and it is all worship. From silence to telling our stories, from Communion to lighting candles, from prayers to Scripture reading, from dancing to singing—it is all done as an act of God-centered worship.

Orthodox Symbolism

We use worship elements that are similar to symbolism and mystery as celebrated by the Orthodox Church. We think the Lord's Supper is a big deal. While most Christian traditions certainly take Holy Communion seriously, we don't make it a simple event. Modernism said we have to figure everything out, but around the Table we celebrate mystery. Amid the rhetorical (and actual) battles over the "real presence" of Christ in the Holy Supper, even John Calvin demurred that it was a mystery that he experienced rather than understood.

Around the Table we celebrate mystery.

When we come to our Lord's Table at Sojourn, we are coming to be fed—spiritually. We do more than simply remember what Jesus did for us and gulp down a sugary grape drink after chewing on a perfectly cubed piece of white bread. We want to be fed by the One who invites us to the banqueting table, who is indeed our Host. We join hands with our brothers and sisters in the "one, holy, catholic, and apostolic church" around the world; and we are fed!

At Sojourn we anoint people with oil. We light many candles, and their fragrance is like incense. We project images of icons, crosses, and nature—incorporating Roman Catholic, Orthodox, and Celtic traditions of symbolic representations in worship. We invite artists to express their worship through their particular medium as they proclaim the gospel through their creative work. All of these are proclamations of faith that lift our hearts toward God.

Charismatic

Clearly, a charismatic worship service is experiential. But it is specifically the freedom that I have experienced in this type of worship expression that is attractive to us in our community. I led praise and worship weekly at the Pentecostal college when I was dating my future wife. I asked her why I never saw her during these gatherings and found that it was because she was lying on the floor under a table. Although people were worshiping in a variety of different ways around her, she felt the freedom to simply lie quietly during the service.

At Sojourn, we have not seen the dramatic manifestations of the Holy Spirit that are evident in most charismatic services; but we experience the freedom to express our worship in a variety of ways, in spirit and in truth. Much of this freedom is observed through the posture of worshipers. Some sit, some stand, some lie on the ground, some kneel. We have worshiped in rows, circles, horseshoe shapes, and so on. Some people lift their hands in praise and others sit quietly.

All of these lift our hearts toward God.

Seeker-Sensitivity

For the Sojourn community, seeker-sensitivity means a willingness to go the extra mile to interpret the content and setting of worship for the spiritual explorer. I am convinced that seeker-sensitivity in a postmodern context is different than in the modern context. In a postmodern context what is beneficial for the follower of Jesus is going to be interesting to the spiritual explorer. We don't need to change the content of our worship; we must, however, be sincere and earnest. Our worship must be authentic and provide interpretive points for a spiritual explorer to understand. We believe that the community's worship is our tool for evangelism. We take seriously our call to evangelism and pray that God would use our authentic worship to speak to the spiritual explorer.

Word-Centered

The Protestant tradition holds to the centrality of the proclamation in Christian worship. The starting point is God and God's revealed Word. We draw on the Scriptures not for answers to our felt needs but for being exposed to God and God's story. Many modern churches focus on cognitive behaviorism. That is, learn the right stuff and work on your actions and you will be fine with the Person upstairs.

Being a follower of Jesus is more than conquering and then spewing out a set of propositions as we do for so many school exams. The ability to incur lasting change for ourselves is questionable ("Just try harder . . . "), but we are compelled to believe that we can be changed, that we can experience that which is true, that we can learn about and experience true faith. We believe this happens best in a community worship experience, not by simply downloading facts from the Bible.

When we gather at Sojourn, we read, hear, or see the story of the Christian Scriptures as a community. We discover that the Bible is not primarily a story about us, although it is easy to find ourselves in it. Rather, it is a story about God and God interacting with all of creation (including humans).

The starting point is God and God's revealed Word.

"Taste and see that the LORD is good" Psalm 34:8.

Sometimes the apprehending of the biblical story comes with teaching from an individual, sometimes with the story of an individual's faith journey, sometimes with silence. We come to feast on God's goodness and leave empowered to be Jesus-followers in the world.

My prayer for you as you worship with youth and young adults is to experience a thriving worshiping life in your group.

—Daniel S. White

We come to feast on God's goodness.

Postmodern Worship

"Taste and see that the LORD is good." Psalm 34:8.

Worship Is a Feast for the Senses . . .

A Feast for the Senses

"A revolution is going on in the streets." I heard this declaration as my mom's Ford Pinto slowed to a stop in front of my grade school. The words came over the radio as an advertisement for a new device called the Sony Walkman®. It was the end of the 1970's and this new invention boasted stereo sound that came not from a small transistor radio, but from a personal listening device that could be strapped onto one's belt while roller-skating backward to a funky disco beat.

The technological revolution continues unabated. Babies being born today will never know a time before mass media, McDonald's, MTV, and multitasking. (And who knows what the future holds.) Welcome to a postmodern world where the individual is out and the community is in, where knowledge is relative and real experience dominates, where science is too simplistic and spirituality is the path to real knowledge.

The word that most sums up the postmodern longing is *authenticity*. If one's life is authentic, one experiences many deep relationships, stretches oneself creatively, and strives for a holistic way of living—that is, a faith that weaves every aspect of one's life together to make the whole, not just a sum of parts. If life now presents itself as a banquet at which to feast, then worship and ministry in this postmodern context will surely have to step up to the table in order to meet the needs of those who live in it. Worship can be a feast for the senses that helps postmodern students fully engage and experience God. What an exciting plate of possibilities!

A Challenge to Modernism

The church of Jesus Christ became quite adept at operating according to modernism. Consequently, ministry in a postmodern context will be a challenge. For now, worship and the ministry of the church must be understood in terms of "cross-cultural" ministry. As the modern church encounters postmoderns, the church faces uncharted waters since no proven models for ministry exist, nor is there a clearly defined understanding of a "postmodern person." There are just questions and ideas that should be asked in every age of the church of Jesus Christ:

"A revolution is going on in the streets. . . ."

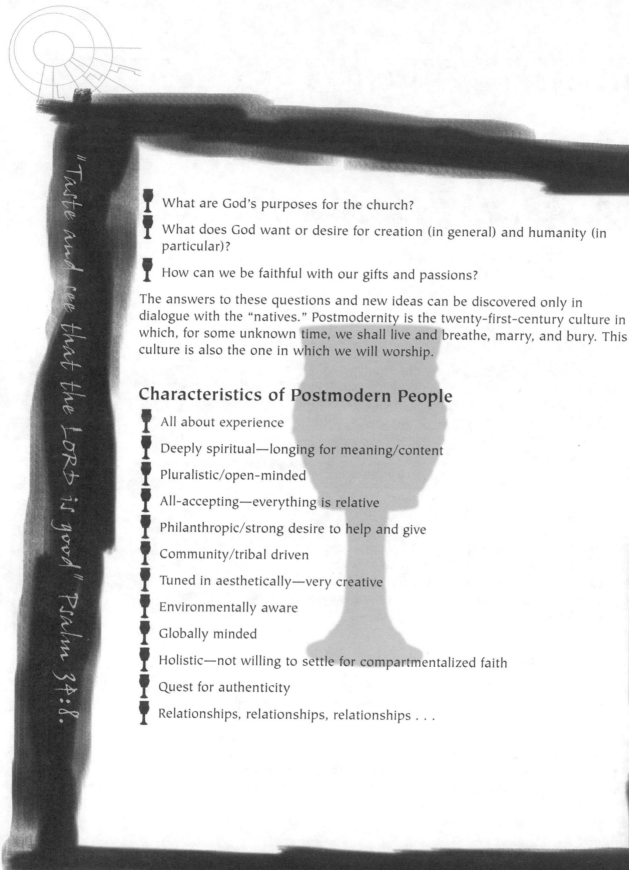

What are God's purposes for the church?

What does God want or desire for creation (in general) and humanity (in particular)?

How can we be faithful with our gifts and passions?

The answers to these questions and new ideas can be discovered only in dialogue with the "natives." Postmodernity is the twenty-first-century culture in which, for some unknown time, we shall live and breathe, marry, and bury. This culture is also the one in which we will worship.

Characteristics of Postmodern People

All about experience

Deeply spiritual—longing for meaning/content

Pluralistic/open-minded

All-accepting—everything is relative

Philanthropic/strong desire to help and give

Community/tribal driven

Tuned in aesthetically—very creative

Environmentally aware

Globally minded

Holistic—not willing to settle for compartmentalized faith

Quest for authenticity

Relationships, relationships, relationships . . .

"Taste and see that the LORD is good" Psalm 34:8.

Worship Is a Feast for the Senses. . . .

What are God's purposes for the church?

Experiential Worship

"Taste and see that the LORD is good" (Psalm 34:8).

A modern take on this psalm might more appropriately be "hear and see that the LORD is good," whereas the postmodern interpretation expands the verse to mean "taste and see and touch and hear and smell"—in other words, experience—"that the LORD is good!" The acquisition and communication of knowledge are important for postmoderns; both are interactive experiences. Consequently, experiential worship is an imperative with which the church must grapple. So what elements create "experiential worship"?

Symbolism

For the last few hundred years (thanks to Gutenberg), the church has been bound by ink-formed letters printed on a page. The wonderful invention of mass publication was a watershed event for Christianity (at least as it flourished in the West); the invention also significantly altered the artistic interpretation and celebration of the Scriptures that had been part of the church for three times as long. Beauty and awe were replaced by logic and codification of biblical facts. Truth, thereafter, became a matter of written proposition.

While the written word still thrives, we can experience truth and beauty through the use of symbols. Stained glass, banners, crosses, icons—these are rich symbols of our tradition through which God's beauty manifests itself. Most modern churches use at least some of these symbols or even others; however, symbols have sometimes become static elements of worship rather than dynamic instruments for encountering the Living God.

Youth who are frustrated by traditional definitions of worship find a way to experience the gospel through projected images and the visual arts. Those who have short attention spans and prefer activity rather than passivity during worship can become artists who create in their own medium as part of the expression of worship. Their artistic expression is both response and proclamation and provides a symbol for the worshiper to grasp and experience.

"Taste and see that the LORD is good" Psalm 34:8.

Worship Is a Feast for the Senses . . .

"Taste and see and touch and hear and smell that the Lord is good."

Multisensory

One need only casually peruse the Book of Leviticus to understand that worship as detailed in the Hebrew Scriptures was not a laid-back endeavor. Incense was offered, prayers were said, ritual washings occurred, and special clothes were worn. Imagine the sights and sounds and smells involved with making a sacrifice.

The Table fellowship of the believers recorded in the Book of Acts was also a sensory experience. According to Acts 2 they not only devoted themselves to the apostles' teaching, but also to sharing a meal together and praying for one another and meeting in the Temple. The image brings to mind, not individuals quietly filing into neat rows set up for them in a bare room, but people gathering together and learning from one another through interaction and dialogue. The picture is a worshiping community that feasts together at God's table. Rather than just taking a single piece of bread and a small sip of wine as we do these days, they filled up on God's goodness.

To be multisensory in our worship is to be biblical. Discussing the Scriptures, lighting incense and candles, hearing testimonies, inviting liturgical dancers to share their gifts, allowing periods of silence—these are good places to start. In the modern era we have so capitalized on the cognitive aspects of worship that we have forgotten how to engage our other faculties in the worship of God. Fabric, flowers, candles, music, images, dance, food—surely these are part of a worship feast. Multisensory worship capitalizes on an ancient-future faith. This expression of worship uses current-day technology and resources in order to engage in ancient forms and movements of Christian worship.

Worship and Mission

To be biblical, the worshiping community also must exist for more than the satisfaction of those persons who attend. Worship is first and foremost about glorifying God through Jesus Christ. Through our worship, God fills us with Christian mission and purpose to bring forth the kingdom of God. Christian community without mission is self-serving; mission without Christian community is public service. Thus, individuals are propelled from the community experience to make a difference in their context of work, school, home, and so on. So for followers of Jesus, the question is: What are we doing as an honest expression of our spirituality? To experience Jesus in a community of worship is an incredible thing, but the experience should motivate us to use our gifts and passions for the good of others and to our Lord's good pleasure.

Multisensory worship capitalizes on an ancient-future faith.

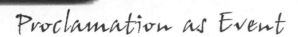

Proclamation as Event

"And the Word became flesh and lived among us, and we have seen his glory . . ." (John 1:14).

A Lived Word

Surely this verse means that Christ was himself a proclamation of God's glory. Yet, he was more than just a spoken Word; he was the Living Word for all to see. Proclamation is more than what we have known it to be in the modern church. For some, "the Word" is preaching: a pastor standing at a pulpit of varying sizes and everyone intently listening to her or him expound on the Scriptures. In other settings it is a highly emotive time when a pastor challenges the congregation through a call and response. For still others, it is the public reading of the Scriptures, the use of liturgical dance, an artistic rendering of a biblical passage. Were not the stained glass windows of so many European cathedrals the only proclamation of the gospel? For worshipers in a postmodern context, proclamation is a lived word, an event—shared testimony, witness, creative arts, dramatic Scripture reading, and yes, even expository sermons.

Concerning the Scriptures

At a recent dialogue in which I participated, a thoughtful Christian author and professor said something to the effect of, "Some people read the Bible not to see what it says, but to affirm what they profess to believe." We are probably all guilty of coming to the Scriptures with an agenda at one time or another. This quotation reminds me that I have not been trained as a pastor to let the Scriptures speak for themselves; rather, I have been trained to explain what they mean to the listener. However, this approach means that the listener may be getting only my side of the story.

Must the Scriptures be explained for them to be powerful? Philip was available for the Ethiopian eunuch at precisely the opportune time to provide understanding and interpretation for him. But Paul indicates that the Scriptures are sharper than a two-edged sword—through the Holy Spirit they expose our sin, teach us God's ways, and comfort us in trials. Some preachers and teachers in a modern context assumed that cognitive apprehension was equal to spiritual growth. But surely at some time we have hidden God's Word in our heart and yet continue to sin against God, other humans, and all of God's good creation.

"Taste and see that the LORD is good" Psalm 34:8.

Worship Is a Feast for the Senses . . .

Proclamation is a lived word, an event.

The ancient practice of *lectio divina* (divine reading) is a method of proclamation that places the weight of meaning for the hearer firmly on the shoulders of the Holy Spirit. The same Scripture is read multiple times, sometimes by different readers, punctuated by silence. The readers and hearers relinquish control and illumination comes, not by our own minds, but by the grace of God. The Scriptures are proclaimed, but no one person is the translator between God and humans. Imagine this proclamation experience in a worship setting. There is power in creating space for the Holy Spirit to teach.

Story

A number of books on how sermons or "talks" are to be prepared have been written in the last century. Seminaries and biblical institutions endeavored to fully prepare women and men for their vocation as preachers and teachers. Usually some attention was given to the use of illustrations to make a point. In postmodernity, the use of story may very well be one of the most effective ways to communicate.

Someone said that the Word became flesh and that we have turned him back into words. Yet Jesus was himself the master storyteller, and he didn't always tell a story simply to illustrate a point. The parable was used to truly communicate—a back and forth style of learning. In modern preaching and teaching, story was used to clarify an abstraction, to make an example, or to illustrate a moral. Yet the church of Jesus Christ has the ultimate storybook as its manual. The Bible is a great story from Genesis to Revelation about God and God's interaction with all creation and God's people. Telling the story of the Scriptures will be a dominant approach to proclaiming the gospel in a postmodern context.

To modern ears the term *story* tends to denote falsehood or myth. However, for the postmodern person, story is reality, life-proven lessons, history and legacy, and something of true meaning. Or better, story is no different from the "facts" of the modern person. If science says one thing, it is acceptable for religion to say another. Paradox, in a postmodern context, is celebrated.

One Side Note

One cannot discuss the issues of story and the proclamation of the Scriptures without delving briefly into the arena of the nature of truth. Jesus said that he was the Life, the Way, and the Truth. Somehow in the modern period truth became

There is power in creating space for the Holy Spirit to teach.

understood to mean a statement or proposition that was incontrovertible. However, Jesus refers to himself not as a proposition, but as Truth embodied. Oftentimes followers of Jesus end up describing faith in terms of accepting a set of propositions. Although propositions can indeed express the contents of faith, they alone are not the content. To say it another way, Jesus-followers believe in a person of God, not in a proposition about God.

Truth must be approached humbly. To think that all postmodern people do not believe in truth is simply naive. For the postmodern person it is more nearly accurate to say that many truths exist.

Context

Finally, proclamation must be understood as a contextual event. What is valuable in Seattle won't necessarily be heard in the same way in the Midwest, nor will what is meaningful in North America be authentic in West Africa. No single postmodern service model exists. Rather, there are models that are discovered through trial and error. Postmodern worship services are a contextually sensitive ministry.

Community

"How good and pleasant it is for sisters and brothers to live together in unity" (Psalm 133:1).

As a Spiritual Reality

Community exists for followers of Jesus before it is—or whether it is— experienced. The apostle John says we have fellowship with one another because our fellowship is in the Son. In other words, it is not because we like one another that we have fellowship; it is a spiritual reality. In his book *Life Together*, Dietrich Bonhoeffer writes about community as experienced in Jesus Christ. He says that Christian community cannot be realized outside of Christ; we are bound to one another only in and through Christ. Surely this is the meaning of community for postmodern persons.

The community experience prompts individuals to make a difference in their context of work, school, home, and so forth.

Experiential Community

Being "a community" involves more than being in the same place at the same time. Experiencing community is more than joining a small group. It has to do with pursuing common purposes and passions, living life, and doing worship together. Christian community is a God-infused sense of togetherness. And yet it is fascinating how frequently that community is experienced and observed without Jesus Christ.

Vladimir Putin was one of the first world leaders to call George W. Bush on September 11, 2001, in response to the shocking and tragic events of that day. This action must have amazed many older Americans. My parents grew up when the threat of nuclear war was a daily concern. Bomb shelters, nuclear fallout plans, and other "cold war" preparations were commonplace. Their parents (as well as their own generation) hated Communist Russia.

Now, Russian presidents call their former foes on the phone and encourage them—as friends. American Presidents rely on their former foes for support and intelligence.

Yet when I ask some postmodern young people why they no longer go to church, the response sounds as if they have observed cold-war politics. They do not understand why so many denominations exist, why they don't work together, why they badmouth one another, and why they don't act like friends. They want to be Christians existing as a true, experiential community.

If "Vlad" and "W" can be friends, surely different churches and different denominations can move away from forced tolerance of one another (at best) and into true partnership, or better yet, Christian community. The unchurched in this postmodern era will not be interested in a divisive and angry pseudo-community; they want to see authentic expressions of Christian community. This community says to everyone, "Don't look at me, look at Jesus." In a postmodern context it is the community of faith and embodied conviction—not the Scriptures themselves—that is, in the final analysis, the meaningful for the gospel.

The Communion of Saints

When a local radio station recently changed its format, I found myself looking forward to my environment-polluting commute more than ever. Their catch-phrase is, "music from the 80's and beyond." So now I listen to retro music, I

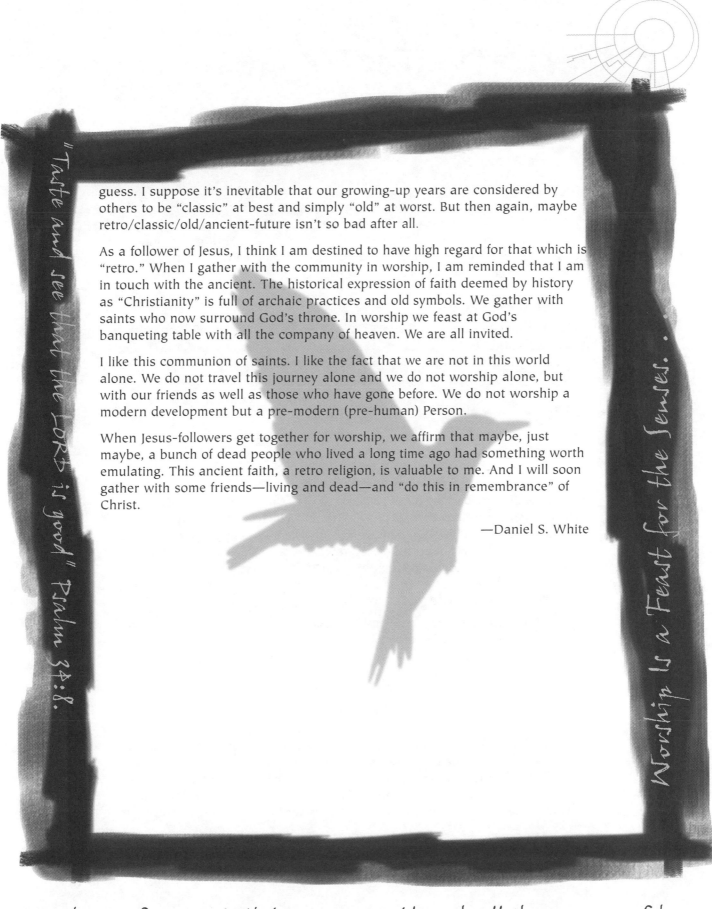

guess. I suppose it's inevitable that our growing-up years are considered by others to be "classic" at best and simply "old" at worst. But then again, maybe retro/classic/old/ancient-future isn't so bad after all.

As a follower of Jesus, I think I am destined to have high regard for that which is "retro." When I gather with the community in worship, I am reminded that I am in touch with the ancient. The historical expression of faith deemed by history as "Christianity" is full of archaic practices and old symbols. We gather with saints who now surround God's throne. In worship we feast at God's banqueting table with all the company of heaven. We are all invited.

I like this communion of saints. I like the fact that we are not in this world alone. We do not travel this journey alone and we do not worship alone, but with our friends as well as those who have gone before. We do not worship a modern development but a pre-modern (pre-human) Person.

When Jesus-followers get together for worship, we affirm that maybe, just maybe, a bunch of dead people who lived a long time ago had something worth emulating. This ancient faith, a retro religion, is valuable to me. And I will soon gather with some friends—living and dead—and "do this in remembrance" of Christ.

—Daniel S. White

Worship Is a Feast for the Senses. . .

In worship we feast at God's banqueting table with all the company of heaven.

Time to Get Started

So what now do you do to begin experiential worship with your group? Worship Feast Services are not prescriptive directions that should be matched exactly. Find freedom between the lines and adapt the services to your specific needs. Your group may not enjoy singing and that's OK. Your group may want to sing more or different songs and that's OK. Be as creative and expressive within your context as your youth will let you go!

Youth-Led Worship

- Gather together a youth worship team to organize, plan, publicize, and lead the worship services.
- Be in ministry with your youth and help them develop their gifts through worship.

Music

- Whatever the musical style of your group, do your best to incorporate it into worship. If you use projected or reprinted lyrics of copyrighted music, be sure to have the appropriate CCLI license.
- If music is not your specialty, invite a musician to help you organize a band or ensemble to lead the music in worship.
- Use music from different traditions and various ethnic sources. If you sing mostly praise and worship choruses, incorporate hymns and chants. If you sing mostly gospel or hip-hop music in worship, try adding some fun bass lines to hymns and choruses. Look on pages 127–128 for a list of great music resources.

Adapt. Adapt. Adapt.

- Again, use these services as a springboard for creativity with the particular gifts and talents of your youth.
- Feel free to use the Orders of Service to create your own handout or bulletin.

The Services

- You'll need readers and musicians for every service. Most calls to prayer, prayers, and benedictions are written for you but feel free to expand them to speak directly to your group. You will probably want to make a handout for each service with the prayers and responsive readings printed on it.
- You'll find sources for music suggestions in the columns and in the index.
- Some services include Holy Communion. You'll want to make sure you have that worked out according to your tradition prior to hosting the worship service.

Worship Is a Feast for the Senses. . . .

The table is ready. Let the feasting begin!

A Night of Prayer

The Experience: A few weeks before scheduling this worship experience, get your group excited about having a prayer service. Prepare the worshipers for a time of silence and meditation. Have one or more leaders act as greeters who will distribute handouts and help the youth enter in silence and quietly find a seat. Throughout the service, simply play music and encourage the participants to be in prayer and meditation. Begin with a call to prayer and close with a benediction.

Environment: Evening; dim lights; several scented candles that are lit; scrolling images of icons, crosses, cathedrals, nature, and saints, as well as some current images (for example: pictures of children praying, images of persons from other countries, persons in hospitals, and so on); meditative music playing

Setup: Arrange rugs and pillows in a semicircle around an altar table. Decorate the altar with candles and rich-colored fabrics. Place the video screens on either side of the table. Provide a few chairs for those who need them.

Senses: *Visuals*—decorated altar and projected images; *sounds*—quiet music and contrast of silence with praying hearts; *smells*—pleasant scents of candles that make the space welcoming; *touch*—quotations handout, posture

Supplies

- Copies of "For Your Meditation" handout (on page 22)
- Candles and matches
- Colored fabric
- Rugs or pillows
- Meditative music (either recorded or by a group of musicians)

Order of Service

Call to Prayer: "Welcome to a night of prayer. As Jesus prayed in the garden, we too are called to prayer. Tonight we will pour our hearts out to God. Do not be afraid of the silence; God is near. You have been given a handout with quotations, Scriptures, and prayers for meditation. If you have trouble stilling your heart and mind to pray, focus your attention on one of the printed items. Listen for God's voice deep within your heart. Now let us pray."

Time for Silent Meditation: Play chant music softly and run the slides.

Benediction: Have everyone rise and hold hands for the benediction: "God's mercies are new every morning, and never fail. May you rest this night in the peace of Christ and wake renewed in your faith and in the great mercies of our living God. Peace be with you. Amen."

For Your Meditation

Quotations

"We should accept with simplicity whatever understanding the Lord gives us; and what [the Lord] doesn't we shouldn't tire ourselves over. For one word of God's will contains within itself a thousand mysteries" (Teresa of Avila [1515–1582], *Meditation on the Song of Songs*).

"Savior, like a shepherd lead us, much we need thy tender care; in thy pleasant pastures feed us, for our use thy folds prepare" (from the hymn "Savior, Like a Shepherd Lead Us," words attributed to Dorothy A. Thrupp, 1836).

"Let us plead for faith alone, faith which by our works is shown; God it is who justifies, only faith the grace applies" (from the hymn "Let Us Plead for Faith Alone," words by Charles Wesley, 1740).

Scriptures

"I lift up my eyes to the hills—from where does my help come? My help comes from the Lord, who made heaven and earth" (Psalm 121:1-2).

"Search me, O God, and know my heart; test me and know my thoughts. See if there is any wicked way in me, and lead me in the way everlasting" (Psalm 139:23-24).

"Surely God is my salvation; I will trust, and will not be afraid, for the Lord God is my strength and my might; [God] has become my salvation" (Isaiah 12:2).

"Do not let your hearts be troubled. Believe in God, believe also in me. In my Father's house there are many dwelling places. If it were not so, would I have told you that I go to prepare a place for you? And if I go and prepare a place for you, I will come again and will take you to myself, so that where I am, there you may be also" (John 14:1-3).

"Peace I leave with you; my peace I give to you. I do not give to you as the world gives. Do not let your hearts be troubled, and do not let them be afraid" (John 14:27).

"God is love, and those who abide in love abide in God, and God abides in them" (1 John 4:16b).

Prayers

Loving God, pour your love into my heart and let it overflow to those around me.

O God who forgives all our sins, forgive me for . . .

There is room in my heart for you, Lord Jesus; come and rule my life.

Waking Up With God

The Experience:
Use this service for morning prayer meetings, or on trips and retreats. Instill in the youth the importance of starting every day by praising God, listening to God's voice, and seeking God's presence. Practice *lectio divina*, an ancient spiritual discipline of reading Scripture reflectively, or praying the Scriptures.

Environment:
Preferably outdoors, in the morning; soft music (optional)

Setup:
Outdoor service: Have everyone get comfortable and spread out within hearing distance; indoor service: Set up pillows around the room for the youth to sit on.

Senses:
Visual—the outdoors, nature; *sounds*—repetition of the same Scripture, silence, and the sounds of nature; *smells*—the freshness of morning air; *touch*—the feel of the ground

Supplies

- Meditative music (optional)

- Rugs or pillows for an indoor service

- Journals and Bibles for the participants

- Pens

Order of Service

Beginning: Sing together a favorite praise chorus or hymn.

Lectio Divina Reading: Use Psalm 5:1-3, about praying in the morning (or another chosen Scripture passage). After each reading, have "sacred pauses" so that the youth have time to experience the "holiness" of the Scripture.

Invite the participants to close their eyes and focus on their breathing. Tell the youth that you are going to read a passage through three times.

1st Reading: Say: "As I read aloud the passage this first time, just listen to the text. Don't analyze the words; simply listen to them." [Read the text, followed by a pause.]

2nd Reading: Say: "As I read the passage this time, try to feel the words—what do you see, what do you hear, what images come to your mind, what tastes do you experience?" [Read the text, followed by a pause.]

3rd Reading: Say: "As I read the passage one last time, envision yourself and God together in the scene you just imagined. What does God say to you?" [Read the text, followed by a pause.]

After the readings, have an extended period of silence in which the worshipers can be alone with God, their journals, and their Bibles. Encourage the participants to reflect on what God might be saying to them through the Scripture and the silence.

Closing: Come back together. Close with prayer requests and sing another chorus.

23

Supplies

- Small beads, lacing, bells, keyrings
- Candles and matches
- Clay
- Fabric strips (about 2 by 6 inches)
- Crayons
- Fish net
- Markers
- Masking tape
- Large sheets of paper or posterboard
- Construction and white paper
- Pens, pencils
- Polished rocks, sand
- Large container, such as a wading pool
- Stapler or tape
- Pictures of children sponsored by your church through an organization such as World Vision, of a family you served on a work trip, or of people from a mission site your church sponsors
- Hymnals or songbooks containing your selected songs

3 Concert of Prayer: A Prayer Station

The Experience: Many Korean churches practice *Tongsung Kido,* a tradition in which the entire congregation prays aloud at the same time. This powerful experience symbolizes the constant chorus of prayer that is happening around the world at any moment. This service is an adaptation of *Tongsung Kido* in that the youth will be praying silently at different prayer stations around the worship space.

Help the participants learn that talking and listening to God occur through different forms and by using all our senses. In addition to introducing some new ways to pray, lead the youth in a meaningful experience of prayer as worship.

Environment:
The participants will explore these prayer stations and activities:
- The Joyful Noise Zone (Make jewelry or keychains that make noise.)
- The Caring Corner (Pray about giving money to support needy children.)
- The Prayer Chain Zone (Link one's prayers with the prayers of others.)
- The Crayon Zone (Remember the simplicity of childhood.)
- The Friendship Soul Zone (Give thanks for good friends.)
- The Graffiti Zone (Remember that we are made in God's image.)
- The Knotty Zone (Discover that God frees us from "knotty" problems.)
- The Potters' Soul Zone (Consider God's handiwork while molding clay.)
- The Real Rock Cafe (Stand on God, our Rock.)
- The Sand Pit Soul Zone (Bury one's burdens deep in the sand pit.)

Setup

- You will need a flexible space, such as a fellowship hall, where tables and chairs can be set up and items can be taped to the walls.

- Create the prayer station signs. If possible, print them on 11 by 17 paper so they can be read more easily. Use dowels and coffee cans filled with gravel to make the signs free-standing, or hang them on the walls. Copy onto the signs the instructions for each station (see pages 26–27).

- Set the prayer stations up around the room with plenty of room between each center.

- Dim the lights and have scented candles lit around the room.

Senses:
Visuals—prayer stations; *sounds*—silence and praise music; *smells*—candles; *touch*—various activities at the stations

Order of Service

Prelude: As people arrive, have some soft, meditative music playing. Distribute "The Breath Prayer" handout (page 28) and allow the participants a few minutes to experience this form of prayer.

Greeting: "This service features a variation on a Korean form of prayer, *Tongsung Kido*, in which the entire congregation prays aloud at the same time. We will pray silently at the same time at various prayer stations. Prayer is not just a verbal event. Many ways to pray use all our senses to help us communicate with God. Use this time to tell God anything that is on your heart; also listen for the quiet voice of God within. For God to communicate with us, we must be open and receptive to the ways the Spirit moves within us. Stand for our opening song."

Songs: One or more prayer songs ("Have Thine Own Way, Lord"; "Sanctuary"; "O Lord, Hear My Prayer" [Taizé]).

Scripture: James 5:13-16 (*the prayer of faith*)

Introduction to the Prayer Stations: "Notice the prayer stations set up around the room. Visit them in any order, spending as much or as little time as you wish at each one. If one station is crowded, try another one. When you hear the signal [or distinct change of music], finish what you are doing and gather again in the center of the room. Please do these activities in silence so as not to disrupt the prayers of others."

(*Allow about forty-five minutes for the prayer station visits. Play meditative music from a CD in the background. Use your signal to call everyone back together.*)

Unison Prayer: (projected or printed)

"Now let us join our voices as one as we pray: 'O God of all creation, we come here today because we yearn for a connection with you. We want to feel your presence in our lives, to hear your voice with new ears, and to know how we can serve you better. We want to be completely changed by our relationship with you. Like the clay we shaped with our hands, mold us into living symbols of your love. Like the pit in which we buried our burdens and sins, may our hearts contain an abundance of joy and forgiveness for others. Teach us how to pray and how to live—make them one and the same. We pray these things in the name of Jesus, the one whom you chose to connect us to you. Amen.' "

Song: Close with a favorite praise song.

Benediction: "Go out into the world, and make prayer for the world a vital part of your life. Go out into the places you live, and make your life your prayer. Amen."

Prayer Stations

The Joyful Noise Zone: "Make a joyful noise to the Lord, all the earth. Worship the Lord with gladness; come into [God's] presence with singing" (Psalm 100:1-2).

What makes you joyful? How do you praise God? Celebrate God's presence in your life by making jewelry or a keychain with the bells and the rope that you find in the Joyful Noise Zone. Then wear your jewelry this week to remind you to make a joyful noise to the Lord wherever you go. Every time you hear the bells jingle, thank God for someone or something in your life.

The Caring Corner: "What does the Lord require of you but to do justice, and to love kindness, and to walk humbly with your God?" (Micah 6:8).

What do the pictures represent for you? Remember the need of the persons in the photos? Do not forget those who have little. These pictures represent only a few of the millions of people around the world who live in poverty or constant need.

Pray for all the hungry children of the world. Ask God what you can do to care for the poor—and be sure to listen closely for God's answer. Make a commitment here to give some portion of your money each month to help support needy families. If each of us puts in just a dollar or two each month, we can make a huge difference. If you can do so today, put some money in the jar. Our care for them is part of our prayer for them . . . and part of God's answer to their prayers.

The Prayer Chain Zone: "I do not cease to give thanks for you as I remember you in my prayers" (Ephesians 1:16).

Prayer links us to God and to one another. Praying for other people is one of the most powerful ways that we can help them. Think about people in your life and anything they may need help with. As you pray for them, write their names on strips of paper. Then tape them together and add them to the chain. Joining your prayers with those of others can help link all of us more closely to God. Make as many "links" as you want.

The Crayon Zone: "[Jesus] said, 'Truly I tell you, unless you change and become like children, you will never enter the kingdom of heaven' " (Matthew 18:3).

Remember how easy life was when you were a little kid? Try to recapture the simplicity of your childhood. Think about the things that were important to you as a kid—being safe, being loved, loving others. Think about the things that made you happy—blowing bubbles, playing with a puppy, sleeping over at a friend's house. Draw a picture to remind yourself of God's steadfast love for you throughout your life.

The Friendship Soul Zone: "We loved you so much that we were delighted to share with you not only the gospel of God but our lives as well because you had become so dear to us" (1 Thessalonians 2:8, NIV).

Think about the friends who are important to you. We get to know God better through knowing other believers and through being part of a Christian community. Think about all your friends, but especially those who share in your life of faith. Use the paper and scissors that are here to cut out shapes that represent your friends in faith. Add your shapes to the collage so you can see how far our Christian community extends.

The Graffiti Zone: "So God created humans in God's own image . . . male and female, God created them" (Genesis 1:27).

God's image is in all of us. Maybe God's image is seen in your light spirit, your laughter, and your jokes. It could be reflected in your caring touch and willingness to listen. Or maybe you are like God in your strength and your ability to share others' burdens.

Think now about how God's image is reflected in you. Use the graffiti walls to express what you've discovered. You might do this by drawing a picture, writing a poem or prayer, or just signing your name. What matters is that you begin to see God at work in your life.

The Knotty Zone: "In everything, by prayer and petition, with thanksgiving, present your requests to God" (Philippians 4:6).

When you run into a "knotty" problem, God is always there to help you out. Think about your life and ask for God's guidance. With God's grace and strength, you can face anything that comes along. For each of your prayers, take a strip of fabric and tie it to the fishnet, giving your concerns to God. Let God free you of worry; then go out in the knowledge that you are not alone, but that you are held and supported in the net of God's grace.

The Potters' Soul Zone: "Just like the clay in the potter's hand, so are you in my hand" (Jeremiah 18:6).

Potters will tell you that clay sometimes seems to have a life of its own. But in the right hands it can be shaped and molded into something beautiful.

Pick up some clay and begin to work with it in your hands. Feel the qualities of the clay itself. Then notice how you can mold it into various shapes. Invite God to guide your hands as you work with the clay to create something new. Think about how God shapes our lives, working with us as we are, yet helping us to become more spiritually alive. Shape the clay into something you can take with you as a reminder of your own relationship with the divine Potter.

The Real Rock Cafe: "Trust in the Lord forever, for in the Lord God you have an everlasting rock" (Isaiah 26:4).

Read the verse on the large rock. It describes three qualities of God—as a solid foundation for our lives, a protector, and one who saves us. Find a small rock that interests you. As you feel and study the rock, think of ways God has been a rock, a fortress, and/or a deliverer in your life. Give thanks to God for being your rock, and take your small rock with you to put in your pocket daily as a reminder of God our Rock.

The Sand Pit Soul Zone: "Cast all your anxiety on [God] because God cares for you" (1 Peter 5:7).

When you really feel "in the pits" about something, do you ever wish you could just bury your problems? Spend some time in God's presence. The candles are symbols that Christ is here with you. On a piece of paper, write down any problems that you want to turn over to God. Do not put your name on the paper—this is between you and God. Then bury it deep in the sand, knowing that God sees and forgives and will help you deal with whatever is troubling you.

Chapter 1: Prayer Services

The Breath Prayer

In the Hebrew Bible, the word for *spirit* is the same as the word for *breath*. A breath prayer is an ancient form of prayer in which our breathing and our needs shape our prayer. A traditional form of the prayer—spoken rhythmically as you inhale and exhale—consists of these words: *"Lord Jesus Christ, Son of God, have mercy on me, a sinner."* Either use this phrase, or create your own prayer by combining words or phrases from each column below, filling in words like *to* or *with* as necessary. Then simply repeat the phrase with each breath, relaxing and focusing your mind and body on the One who gives you breath.

Name for God	Verb	What You Desire
Lord	*fill me*	*your peace*
Holy God	*help me*	*live for you*
Compassionate One	*guide me*	*know your will*
Holy Spirit	*mold me*	*see the world as you do*
Jesus Christ	*show me*	*understanding*
Heavenly Parent	*grant me*	*patience*
Healing God	*give me*	*strength for the journey*
Giver of Life	*touch me*	*joy*
Father	*lead me*	*your love*
Creator	*send me*	*courage*

Scripture and Reflection

The Experience: This service focuses on hearing the voice of the Lord. As with the ancient practice of *lectio divina*, here the emphasis is on reading and hearing the Scriptures and then reflecting on what the Spirit is saying through them. In this case the community reads in unison the Scripture, observes silence concluded by a sung response, and finally celebrates Holy Communion as an act of thanksgiving.

Environment: Make a cross on the floor out of candles and place rugs or pillows around the room. The atmosphere of the service should transmit the idea of being at the foot of the cross. Let the candles give light and a scented aroma to the room.

Setup: Chairs and/or rugs in a semicircle around the cross; worship band or instrumentalists in rear of room; silence; a video screen placed on one side of the cross for words of music and Scriptures; several unlit candles at the front of the worship space along with lighting sticks (the participants will light the candles when the service begins)

Senses: *Visuals*—cross, projected Scriptures; *sounds*—unison voices, music, silence; *smells*—candles; *touch*—posture of worship; *tastes*—bread and juice

Supplies

- Candles and matches
- Rugs or pillows
- Bibles
- Recorded music or musicians
- Slides or transparencies of Scriptures
- Taizé songs found in *Songs From Taizé* (ISBN: 2850401285)
- "God of Wonders," found on *City on a Hill: Songs of Worship and Praise CD*• "Better Is OneDay," found on *Passion: OneDay Live*

Order of Service

Greeting: "God is here waiting for us. Let us listen. Let us seek. Let us linger in the glow of Christ our Lord. [Band begins playing music.] Come and light a candle signifying your desire to experience the light of Christ."

Praise and Worship:	"Better Is OneDay" and "God of Wonders"
Corporate Scripture Reading:	Psalm 84:1-4 (*Longing to be in God's presence*)
Silent Reflection	
Response:	"O Lord, Hear My Prayer" [Taizé]
Corporate Scripture Reading:	Psalm 84:5-7 (*God's strength is above all*)
Silent Reflection	
Response:	"O Lord, Hear My Prayer"
Corporate Scripture Reading:	Psalm 84:8-12 (*Living in God's courts*)
Silent Reflection	
Response:	"O Lord, Hear My Prayer"

The Celebration of Holy Communion: (*Talk about Communion as an act of spending time in God's presence.*)

Response:	"Better Is OneDay"

Blessing: "We have spent a moment in time here at the feet of God. Now go and live your lives in the presence of God. Amen."

29

Seek and Find

Supplies

- Bibles

- "Seek Ye First," found in most hymnals or songbooks

The Experience: Postmodern youth find truth in mosaic form. Storytelling and drama communicate the gospel message in a fresh way. Use this time to encounter God through story and visual imagery. This service includes a drama, a guided imagery prayer, and a folk-tale along with Scripture and traditional hymns.

Environment: Set a tone of welcome and hospitality. The service can be used for a youth Sunday, or for your regular worship times.

Setup: Arrange chairs (or sit on the floor) in a circle. Make sure to have ample space for the drama. You will need different readers (*assign these parts ahead of time so that the volunteers can rehearse*). Have recorded music or a band prepared.

Senses: *Visuals*—drama; *sounds*—responsive readings, music, guided meditation

Order of Service

Call to Worship

LEADER: O God, you are my God; I seek you.

PEOPLE: **My soul thirsts for you.**

LEADER: My flesh faints for you as in a dry and weary land where there is no water.

PEOPLE: **I have looked upon you in the sanctuary,**

LEADER: beholding your power and glory,

PEOPLE: **because your steadfast love is better than life.**

LEADER: My lips will praise you.

PEOPLE: **I will bless you as long as I live.** (Psalm 63:1-4)

Song of Preparation: "Seek Ye First"

Drama: "Seek and Find" (page 33)

The Gospel Reading: Matthew 6:25-34 (*Do not worry.*)

The Hebrew Bible Reading: Jeremiah 29:13 (*Search and find God.*)

30

(Play meditative, instrumental music in the background. Tell the participants to take a deep breath, hold it, and release it [repeat three times] if they begin to feel restless during the prayer. The pauses [marked by points of ellipses] should last about ten to twenty seconds.)

Call to Prayer: "In this time we are going to pray that God would teach us to really pray. First, we will pray in meditation. This type of prayer seeks to reach into your imagination to discover spiritual truth. God works through every aspect of our being—our heart, our mind, and our imagination. There is no right or wrong response. If you relax so much you fall asleep, even that is OK. Go with whatever thoughts and ideas come to you. Don't try to manipulate the story; accept the first images that come to mind. The only 'rules' are that you may not disturb others. Find a comfortable spot where you can relax and where you are not touching anyone else. Also, please remain silent and respect everyone's opportunity to experience this type of prayer."

A Guided Imagery Prayer: "Take a deep breath in, hold it, and release. Another deep breath, hold, release. Close your eyes and begin to relax; let go of any tension in your body. Take a deep breath in, hold it, and release. Another deep breath, hold, release. Feel the warmth spreading down from your head, relaxing all your facial muscles as it flows down your body. Let any tension in your neck and shoulders melt out of your body. Feel this warmth spread down your arms into your hands and then the tips of your fingers. If you feel tension anywhere in your body, picture this warmth helping you release tension and relax. Envision the warmth flowing down your spine, relaxing each vertebra. Take a deep breath in, hold it, and release. Feel your legs relax, your knees, your feet, even your toes. Rest, relaxing in this warmth. Take a deep breath in, hold it, and release.

"Envision yourself on a journey to find a treasure. . . . What are you wearing?. . . . You have a backpack; what color is it?. . . . What have you packed in this bag?. . . . You start your own journey. You begin on a path. . . . What does it look like? . . . What do you see around you? Is the path difficult or easy? steep or straight? . . . What sounds do you hear as you walk down this path? . . . You hear someone walking toward you. . . . What does this person look like? . . . Is it a stranger or someone you know? . . . The person hands you something for your journey; what is it? . . . The stranger disappears and you continue on your journey. . . . Something blocks the path. . . . What is it? . . . You use something in your pack or whatever the person gave you to continue your journey. . . . You sense that you are getting closer to the treasure you seek. . . . What are you feeling? . . . What do you hope to find? . . . Something in your pack or whatever the person gave you contains a clue for finding your treasure. . . . What is it? . . . If the clue doesn't come right away, be patient; it will. Use this clue to find your treasure. . . . Now that you found your treasure, what will you do with it? . . .

"Come back to this time and place, but keep your eyes closed. Relax for a while in God's presence and love [*pause for at least thirty seconds to one minute*]. Now ask God any questions you may have and then listen [*pause for at least thirty seconds to one minute*]. Now bring into your heart all those you love and feel God's love surround them [*pause for at least thirty seconds to one minute*]. Let the other people slowly fade. If there is anything else you want to share with God, do so now [*pause for at least thirty seconds to one minute*]. Know that you are a child of God, created to be you, loved unconditionally. Live in this love. Join me in praying the Lord's Prayer." [*Turn off the music.*]

31

A Story Message: "An old folk-tale is told about a Christian community that had fallen into discontent; rivalry, criticism, and jealousy were prevalent. The members of the community could agree on nothing. Everything was a point of conflict. Each was envious of the others—of their homes, their families, and their possessions. They couldn't agree on a leader and there was no vision. 'Where there is no vision, the people perish' (Proverbs 29:18; King James Version).

"A rumor arose that a wise rabbi lived in the nearby woods, so a group of people went out to question him as to the secret of a happy life. They went as a group, because there was such mistrust in the community. The rabbi simply said: 'The Messiah has come and he lives in your community.' The people were all puzzled. They certainly hadn't seen the Messiah, or had they? They went back to the rest of the community and told them what the wise rabbi had said.

"The change was gradual, as each person began to look at his or her neighbors differently. Could he be the Messiah? Do you think she is the Messiah? The first noticeable difference was that people who hadn't spoken to each other in years began to say hello and nod and smile. Soon they were talking to one another. People began to give to those in need. Laughter was again heard in homes and in the streets. Kindness and forgiveness became the order of the day as each person looked at the other, wondering—is this the Messiah? Genuine love and care warmed the hardest of hearts. The community was transformed into what it had originally been intended to be. The rabbi was a very wise man."

Affirmation:

"Seek the Lord while he may be found, call upon [the Lord] while he is near" (Isaiah 55:6).

Closing Hymn:

"Seek Ye First"

Benediction:

"So if you have been raised with Christ, seek the things that are above where Christ is seated at the right hand of God" (Colossians 3:1). Amen.

Seek and Find Drama

(Two strangers are sitting on a park bench. The brief dialogue is packed with meaning. Pay close attention to the inflections of each line.)

SPEAKER 1: Nice day.
SPEAKER 2 (*incredulous*): What?

SPEAKER 1: Nice day.
SPEAKER 2: Not really.

Speaker 1: No?
SPEAKER 2: No.

SPEAKER 1: Hungry?
SPEAKER 2: No thanks.

SPEAKER 1: You sure?
SPEAKER 2: Well. . . .

SPEAKER 1: (*mimes sharing a box of popcorn*): **Here.**
SPEAKER 2 (*points to his heart*): No, here.

SPEAKER 1 (*taken aback*): **Oh!**
SPEAKER 2: Well?

SPEAKER 1 (*unsure*): **Well . . . ah . . .**
SPEAKER 2: Never mind.

SPEAKER 1: No, wait.
SPEAKER 2: Why?

SPEAKER 1: Truth?
SPEAKER 2: Yours?

SPEAKER 1: No. Hope?
SPEAKER 2 (*sarcastically*): Right.

SPEAKER 1: Love!
SPEAKER 2: Whose?

SPEAKER 1 (*pointing upward*): **His.**
SPEAKER 2: How?

SPEAKER 1: Ask.
SPEAKER 2: For?

SPEAKER 1: Forgiveness.
SPEAKER 2: Find?

SPEAKER 1: Grace.
SPEAKER 2: Receive?

SPEAKER 1: Life!
SPEAKER 2: Too easy.

SPEAKER 1: Yeah!
SPEAKER 2: No way.

SPEAKER 1: Way. Truth. Life.
SPEAKER 2: You're sure?

SPEAKER 1: Yep.
SPEAKER 2: OK.

SPEAKER 1: OK?
SPEAKER 2: Yeah!

SPEAKER 1: Nice day.
SPEAKER 2: Great day!

Teach Me to Pray

Supplies

- Bibles

- Music

- Plastic balls for ACTS prayer

- All songs are found in most hymnals or songbooks.

The Experience: Use this worship service to teach your group how to pray. Some of the skits are serious, some are exaggerations; but the worship time as a whole is a great way to help your youth feel comfortable praying both in private and aloud. After the skits, pray together using the ACTS model for prayer.

Environment: Sit in a semicircle shape; reserve enough space to do the skits.

Setup: Assign readers ahead of time for the various skits. Memorization of the parts is recommended, but simply reading them aloud will do.

Senses: *Visuals*—skits; *sounds*—dramatic voices, music, friends praying; *touch*—ACTS prayer activity

Order of Service

Call to Worship: Play "Sweet Hour of Prayer" in the background. Have four readers speak the Lord's Prayer (page 36) from four different positions in the room.

Praise and Worship:　　　　"As the Deer"

　　　　　　　　　　　　　　　"Change My Heart, O God"

　　　　　　　　　　　　　　　"Seek Ye First"

　　　　　　　　　　　　　　　"Near to the Heart of God"

A Prayer Drama:　　　　　　"Lord, Teach Us to Pray" (pages 37–38)

Song:　　　　　　　　　　　"Thy Word Is a Lamp"

Scripture Reading:　　　　　Matthew 6:1-8 (*Genuine prayer*)

(*Invite the participant who reads this Scripture aloud to relate his or her personal experiences of prayer following the reading of the Word. If you choose to do so, give several or all of the group members a chance to also tell one of their prayer experiences.*)

Preparing to Pray:　　　　　"Spirit of the Living God"

　　　　　　　　　　　　　　　"Humble Thyself in the Sight of the Lord"

34

ACTS OF PRAYER

Say: "Many of you are familiar with the ACTS pattern for prayer. A stands for *adoration*, C for *confession*, T for *thanksgiving*, and S for *supplication*. We will now participate in an active prayer experience. Let us pray.

[For Adoration] "Think of the word or words you most often use when you name God in prayer. Tell that name to both the person on your left and the person on your right as a form of naming God and demonstrating your adoration."

[For Confession] "If you have something to confess, stand up. This could be either something personal, or something we need to confess as a church, a nation, a people. I will throw a ball to one person, who will state his or her confession and then throw the ball to the next person in line who is standing. Sit down after you have thrown the ball. The last person to speak throws the ball back to me."

[For Thanksgiving] "I will throw several balls to the group. If the ball comes to you, call out something for which you are thankful and then throw the ball to someone else. Together we will create a great noise of joyful thanksgiving. Keep throwing the balls until I say to stop. At that point, please return the balls to the front." (*Have assistants ready to recover any balls that go astray. At the end of this exercise, the helpers are to quickly gather all the balls and put them away.*)

(*Play meditative music in the background for the remainder of this prayer time.*)

[For Supplication] "The act of supplication involves praying for the needs of others. During this time, stand and name a person or situation for which you request prayer. Keep the information general rather than too detailed or specific. If you cannot or prefer not to reveal names or relate the circumstances, just stand quietly."

(*When all the requests have been heard and acknowledged, have everyone stand and continue with this prayer:*)

"Lord, we lift to you these many requests, both the spoken and the unspoken ones. Thank you for being a God who cares about us and hears our prayers. An important part of prayer that we often forget or don't take time for is listening. In these next few minutes, we open our hearts and minds to you. In the stillness of this hour, we listen for you. We wait. Come to us."

End the time of prayer by singing The Doxology.

Benediction (*recited in unison*): "The Lord bless you and keep you; the Lord make his face to shine upon you, and be gracious to you; the Lord lift up his countenance upon you, and give you peace" (Numbers 6:24-26).

The Lord's Prayer

SPEAKER 1:	He was praying in a certain place; and after he had finished one of his disciples said to him,
SPEAKER 2:	"Lord, teach us to pray as John taught his disciples."
SPEAKER 3:	He said to them, "When you pray, say Our
SPEAKER 4:	Father
SPEAKER 1:	Mother
SPEAKER 2:	Friend
SPEAKER 1:	Mentor
SPEAKER 3:	who is in heaven.
SPEAKER 4:	Hallowed be your name.
SPEAKER 1:	Your kingdom come.
SPEAKERS 3 and 4:	Your will be done on earth as it is in heaven.
SPEAKER 2:	Give us each day our daily bread
SPEAKER 3:	and forgive us our sins
SPEAKERS 1 and 2:	as we ourselves forgive those who sin against us.
SPEAKER 4:	Lead us not into temptation
SPEAKER 1:	but deliver us from evil,
ALL SPEAKERS:	for yours is the kingdom
SPEAKER 3:	and the power
SPEAKER 2:	and the glory
SPEAKER 1:	forever
SPEAKERS 3 and 4:	and forever.
ALL SPEAKERS:	Amen."

Lord, Teach Us to Pray

Chad: O Lord, I come to you today from my little corner of the world—the Northern Hemisphere, the United States of America, the great state of [your state], surrounded by the [feature of your state]. Yes, I come to you from Packard Street. I want to bring to your attention that my neighbor, Mrs. Ingram, has been in the hospital for a week. I think she's at the university hospital, not St. Joe's. I believe she is in Room 241. Mrs. Ingram is all alone in the world. Her husband passed on three years ago and just last month her daughter died; so there is no one to care for her now, except me. The other neighbors just don't seem to show any concern for her. I pray that you will help her to not feel so lonely. . . . Today's the big game. I'll be there in my usual seat, right at the fifty-yard line. Wouldn't mind if we won. . . . I'm not sure what exactly ails Mrs. Ingram; but if I find out in the next couple days, I'll let you know. Amen.

Next Scene

Mother: It's time for supper. Would someone please offer grace?
Child 1: We got bread and we got meat, why the dickens don't we eat?
Child 2: Rub a dub dub, thanks for the grub.
Mother: Would someone please offer a serious prayer?
Father: O Almighty Oneness, we beseech thee, lookest down uponst us and grant unto us, hitherto unbeknownst to thee, thy humble children, thankfulness of being for what hast been bestowed uponst us for four score and seven years, brought forth on this continent as a new consideration, when the force was with us before E.T. phoned home to the land of the free and the home of the brave.
Everyone: Amen!
Mother: Thank you. (*The children look a bit puzzled.*)

Next Scene

Maria: OK, God. Like, I have this *huge* crush on Drew and he, like, never seems to notice me. And then today at lunch, I dropped my tray, right in front of him, in front of the whole school, like, omigod (oops, sorry!). Well, he was, like, so nice and helped me pick up the mess and he, like, notices me! I'm about to drop dead (it's just a figure of speech, so don't get any ideas). Well, along comes Jennifer and she, like, tosses her hair and bats her eyelashes at Drew. And he, like, asks her out to the football game Friday night. Like, omigod (sorry, I did it again), right in front of me! So I was thinkin' since you're on my side and all, couldn't you just, like, break her leg? (*long pause*) Maybe if that's, like, too drastic, just make sure she has a bad-hair day! That would be great!

Next Scene

Tony: Dear Father in heaven, I really need the car Saturday night. If I could have the car that night, I'll go to Sunday school and youth group; I'll even attend church. You see, McKenzie

FROM WORSHIP FEAST: 50 COMPLETE MULTISENSORY WORSHIP SERVICES FOR YOUTH. © 2003 by Abingdon Press.

finally said yes! I have a date with her Saturday night. So if I could have the car, I. . . . I will . . . dedicate my life to your service. I'll . . . go to seminary and become a minister. It's the most important date I've ever had and I just have to have the car; or maybe I'll be a missionary to the natives of Bongo Bongo and live in abject poverty. Really, this means so much to me. If you could just convince my parents to loan me the car, I'll do *anything*! Thank you, Lord. Amen. . . . Dad, can I have the car Saturday night?

Father: Sure, just remember that we expect you to get up and go to church with us Sunday morning.

Tony: Why can't you just give me the car? Why do you always try to bargain with me?

Next Scene

Sam: O God, you are well aware of my work for you. I am your dedicated servant. I attend church faithfully every Sunday. I have served as the church council president for fifteen years. I chaired the all-church rummage sale three years in a row. I serve meals to the homeless. I have filled countless missionary barrels with old clothing, canceled stamps, and used tea bags. I have taught junior high Sunday school for twenty-eight years—that alone deserves a nice reward. So please let me win the lottery. Amen.

Next Scene

Kirk and Teammates: OK guys, let's pray! . . . God, this is a really big game. (*Teammates echo, "Yes!"*) Brother Andrew's is a better team and a bigger team. I mean, look at those guys—it's David and Goliath all over again. We know that you are often on the side of the underdog; well, "Underdogs 'R Us!" (*Teammates murmur, "Yes!"*) So God, you must be on our side! (*Teammates exclaim, "Yes!"*) Let's face it; we always lose to them, so we figure it's our turn. That's only fair, you know. So help us wipe them out. (*Teammates shout, "Yes!"*) Help us smash them into oblivion! (*louder "Yes!"*) Let's hurt someone! (*even louder "Yes!"*) Help us annihilate them! (*All the teammates yell, "Yes!" at the top of their lungs.*) . . . (*softly*) In Jesus' name we pray. Amen.

Next Scene

Child: (*speaking extremely slowly*) Now I lay me down to sleeeeeeeeeeeeeep.

Mother: It's late; could you please hurry a bit?

Child: I pray the Looooord, my soul to keeeeeeeeeeeeeeeep.

Mother: Anna, you are stalling; get on with the prayer.

Child: If I should diiiiiiiiie before . . . AM I GOING TO DIE?

Mother: No, you are not going to die; finish the prayer.

Child: If I should die before I wake . . . ARE YOU SURE I'M NOT GOING TO DIE BEFORE I WAKE?

Mother: Will you calm down? Anna, you are not going to die and you are not going to lose your soul. Now GO TO SLEEP!

Child: If I'm not going to die and I'm not going to lose my soul, then why do we pray that?

Mother: We don't really mean it; we just say it because it's a prayer.

Child: (*almost crying, definitely scared*) If I should die before I wake, I pray the Lord my soul to take. I'M GOING TO DIE AND SOMEONE IS GOING TO TAKE MY SOUL! I DON'T WANT TO LOSE MY SOUL!

Mother: Just finish the prayer and go to sleep.

Prayer Drums

The Experience: Say your prayers to the beat of a drum in this worship service. Youth will put their whole bodies into this time of prayer as they beat a rhythm that expresses their joys, concerns, needs, wants, and praises. Gather into a circle and invite one person to begin the drumming; then everyone joins in to his or her own beat.

Environment: Enough space for a large circle, but a room that will fill up with sound; a welcoming and kind atmosphere

Setup: Provide a drum for each participant. (They do not have to be the same size or sound—kids' toy drums work fine.) Some of the youth could bring their own drum. If you cannot find enough drums, use some tambourines, bells, cymbals, woodblocks, or other percussion instruments. Arrange a circle of chairs with a single candle on a table in the center. Set one instrument on each chair and let the youth choose their seats.

Senses: *Visuals*—drums, friends joyfully drumming, lit candle; *sounds*—various sounds of percussion; *touch*—beating or tapping drums

Supplies

- Drums or other percussion instruments
- Candle and matches
- Bible

Order of Service

Opening: Read aloud Psalm 150 (*praise God with instruments*) in unison three times. Each time read louder and faster. When you reach verse six the last time through, repeat the verse again five times.

Preparing to Pray: (*Invite a volunteer to read*.) "Lord we praise you. We are here to make a joyful noise. We are here to pray to you. We are here to bring our needs before you. Come and listen. Dance to the beat of our prayers. Be glorified by our praise. Come and listen. Join your heart to ours as we pray. Put your holy rhythm upon us. Come and listen, Lord. Amen."

Prayers of the People: Explain to the participants that they are going to be drumming their prayers. Encourage the worshipers to let the strength of their drumbeat represent the prayers on their hearts. Have one volunteer begin the drumming, then invite the youth one at a time to join in. As they finish their prayers, have the drumbeats fade out until everyone stops drumming.

Closing: (*Invite a volunteer to read*.) "Lord, we know you were here. We know that you are going with us. We know that you have planted your beat in our hearts. We love you. We will dance for you. We will praise you. We will live our lives to your holy rhythm. Amen."

39

Morning Praise and Prayer

Supplies

- Candle or oil lamp

- Hymnals or songbooks

- Bibles

- "Santo, Santo, Santo" is in most hymnals;

- "Give Me Jesus," in hymnals but also on Fernando Ortega's CD *Home*

- "Shout to the Lord," found in *The Faith We Sing* (cross only edition—ISBN: 0687049040)

The Experience: This service is a new take on the classical Order for Morning Praise and Prayer found in most books of worship. If you meet for a weekly prayer breakfast, or other morning meeting, use this service to open the gathering. Encourage the group members to memorize the format, so that it becomes a natural part of your morning times together.

Environment: Outdoors at dawn if possible, or your regular meeting space

Setup: Provide a Bible and a hymnal or songbook. Sit or stand in a circle. Place a candle or oil lamp in the center representing the light of Christ.

Senses: *Visuals*—outdoors, faces of friends, candle or oil lamp; *sounds*—nature, prayers and praise; *smells*—freshness of morning; *touch*—being outdoors

Order of Service

Call to Praise and Prayer: O Lord, open our lips.

Response: And my mouth will declare your praise.

Songs for Morning:
"Santo, Santo, Santo" (*the Spanish version of Holy, Holy, Holy*)

"Give Me Jesus" (*traditional African American spiritual*)

"Shout to the Lord"

Prayer of Thanksgiving: (*Invite a volunteer to offer a prayer.*)

Scripture Reading: Romans 12:1-2 (*God transforms us.*)

Isaiah 55:1-3 (*God calls us to God's self.*)

Praise and Worship: (*Sing some of your favorite praise songs.*)

Prayers of the People: Invite a volunteer to lead in praying for members and needs in your community and in the world. Open the prayers for all the youth to name aloud a concern, closing with "I'm praying, Lord"; all will respond, "Come and listen to me." End the prayers with the Lord's Prayer.

The Blessing: "God's love endures forever. Live in love, taught by Christ and empowered by the Holy Spirit. God has told us 'Good morning.' Let us go and make our morning good. Amen."

Evening Praise and Prayer

The Experience: This service is a new take on the classical Order for Evening Praise and Prayer found in most books of worship. If you meet for a weekly prayer vigil, or other evening meetings, use this service to open the gathering. Encourage the youth to memorize the format, so that it becomes a natural part of your evening times together.

Environment: Outdoors at dusk, or indoors by candlelight

Setup: Little setup is required for evening praise and prayer. You will need a Bible and a hymnal or songbook. You will also need a stick of incense and an incense holder or plate. Sit or stand in a circle and place a candle or oil lamp in the center representing the light of Christ. Set the incense next to the candle.

Senses: *Visuals*—dusk or candlelight, Christ candle, rising smoke from incense, faces of friends; *sounds*—nature, prayers and praise; *smells*—incense and evening

Supplies

- Candle or oil lamp

- Incense and incense holder

- Bibles

- Songbooks for your chosen praise songs

- "From the Rising of the Sun," found in most praise songbooks but also found in *The Faith We Sing* (cross only edition— ISBN: 0687049040)

Order of Service

The Light of Christ: Invite someone to light the Christ candle and say, "Light and peace in Jesus Christ." The group responds, "Thanks be to God."

The Aroma of Prayer: Ask a volunteer to light the incense while someone else reads aloud Psalm 141:1-2 (*prayers like incense*).

Evening Praise:	"From the Rising of the Sun"
Prayer of Thanksgiving:	(*Have a volunteer offer a prayer.*)
Scripture Reading:	Exodus 13:21-22 (*cloud by day, fire by night*)
	Revelation 22:1-5 (*no more night*)

Silence

Praise and Worship:	(*Sing some of your favorite praise songs.*)

Prayers of the People: Invite a volunteer to lead in praying for members and needs in your community and in the world. Open the prayers for all youth to name aloud a concern closing with, "I'm praying, Lord," with all responding, "Come and listen to me." End the prayers with the Lord's Prayer.

The Blessing: "Sleep tonight in the warmth of God's love. Wake renewed in the power of the Holy Spirit. Live in the grace of the Lord Jesus Christ. Amen."

41

10 Prayer Expressions

Supplies

- Six tables
- Paper
- Charcoal crayons
- Clay
- CD player and several CDs
- Hymnals, songbooks
- Pens and pencils
- Paints and brushes
- Large sheet of paper

The Experience: Unleash the creativity in your youth as you encourage them to use their hands in prayer. Set up different creation stations around the room and let the participants draw, mold, dance, sing, journal, and paint their prayers.

Environment: Open space; well-lit room; atmosphere of creativity

Setup: Provide at least six tables, one for each station. For the drawing station, have paper and charcoal. For the molding station, have either a potter's wheel or small chunks of clay to be molded. The dance station needs only open space, a CD player, and a variety of CDs. At the singing station, have hymnals, songbooks, and paper and pens for those who want to write their own song. You may also choose to have various instruments at that station. For the journaling station, have paper and pencils. For the painting station, have a variety of paints and brushes. Hang a large sheet of paper and let the worshipers choose which portion of the banner they will paint.

Senses: *Visuals*—prayer stations; *sounds*—music and creative activity; *smells*—paints, clay; *touch*—prayer stations

Order of Service

Opening: "Welcome to a time of praying with our hands and bodies. We are going to let our creative expressions become our prayers to God. Feel free to let God create in you a work of art. Do not be afraid and do not hold back. Express yourself in prayer."

Prayers: Before you send the youth to the prayer stations, offer this opening prayer: "Lord, you have created us to be creative. We are here to use our creativity in prayer. Come and be with us. Come and create in us. Come and hear our prayers. Amen." (*Explain that the worshipers may visit the stations in any order. They do not have to pray at every station. Encourage the youth to linger in prayer where they feel the most creative.*)

Testimonies: Invite the youth to talk about their experiences and their artwork. Discuss the ease or difficulty with which they prayed through creative expression. Explain that God hears our prayers whether we say them aloud, write them down, dance them, or draw them. God listens.

Closing Prayer: "God be glorified by our prayer expressions. Thank you for the gift of creativity. Let our lives be prayers to you. Amen."

Breaking and Entering

The Experience: Help your group look for the places where God has broken in and entered the world throughout time and realize that God continues to break into and enter our lives through Christ today. Use ancient texts that express God's activity in the world and reveal God's breaking into our hearts through the celebration of Holy Communion. The participants will read Scriptures in unison, have a brief teaching time, and experience silence.

Environment: mostly candlelit; scrolling images of the quotations on page 45, of saints, bread and wine, Jesus, and crosses; chant or meditative music playing

Setup: Place an altar table in the front of a semicircle. Set up rugs, pillows, or chairs around the altar. Position the band behind the semicircle. If possible, have two different screens: one for scrolling images, one for words of songs/Scriptures.

Senses: *Visuals*—candles, projected images, one another; *sounds*—chant music, unison voices, silence; *smells*—aroma of candles

Supplies

- Candles and matches
- Bread and juice
- Video monitors
- Projector
- Computer
- Rugs or pillows to sit on
- "Awesome God" and "Praise You," in *The Faith We Sing* (cross only edition— ISBN: 0687049040)
- "Let It Rain," on Michael W. Smith's *Worship* CD •
- Bible
- *Conversations* CD, by Sara Groves
- Hymnal
- *Oh, God!* DVD or VHS cassette

Order of Service

Welcome: "You are not here as random participants in just any event in time. You are called here, invited here, and led here to worship God. (Band begins playing music.) Come and light a candle to symbolize your presence here. Join your light to the light of Christ and let us worship." (Everyone lights a candle and the singing begins.)

Praise and Worship:
"Let It Rain"
"Awesome God"
"Praise You"

Scripture Reading: John 1:1-5, 10-14 (*The Word became flesh.*)

Song of Preparation: Listen to the song "The Word" by Sara Groves (found on her *Conversations* CD) and invite the worshipers to reflect on the ways in which they have looked to other books and sources of strength when the Word has been there all along. You may also have the band sing this song as a meditation.

The Message: "Breaking and Entering" (See *"Teaching Points,"* on page 44.)

Praise and Worship: "Word of God, Come Down on Earth" (words by James Quinn, 1969; music by Johann R. Ahle, 1664)

Holy Communion: *(Talk about Communion as the ultimate act of God breaking into our lives.)*

Silence and Meditation

The Lord's Prayer

Pray Together: "Amazing God, thank you for breaking into our world and living among us. Thank you for showing yourself to us in both subtle and boisterous ways. Help us to look for you, to keep watch for you, to wait on you, and to know that you are always working in our lives whether we recognize your handiwork or not. You are amazing and we worship you. Be glorified by our worship and by the lives we lead, through Christ our Lord. Amen."

Praise and Worship: The Doxology

Blessing: "Let us go now from this place looking for our next encounter with the living God. May you experience God breaking into your life and making you new, giving you hope, filling you with peace, and pouring love into your heart this week and forever. Amen."

Teaching Points

- Draw from the following examples (from the Old Testament and other sources) to talk about God "breaking into the world":

    —The angel of the Lord and Abraham (Genesis 15–17)

    —Jacob wrestles the angel (Genesis 32:22-32)

    —Moses and the burning bush (Exodus 3–4)

    —Ezekiel and the wheel within a wheel (Ezekiel 1)

    —Show a clip from *Oh God!* with George Burns and John Denver. While this is a 1977 movie, it contains some great scenes of God (played by George Burns) breaking and entering into John Denver's character's life. One of the first scenes with Burns and Denver would be the best to show and discuss. Introduce the theme of God's activity in our lives. (*Make sure that you have a public performance license to show movies on home video; call Christian Video Licensing International at 888-771-CVLI.*)

    —God shows us a part of God's self in all these examples, but even then we do not see the fullness of God—God's glory—until the Word became flesh. We have seen God's glory (John 1:14). The miracle of the Incarnation is that God breaks in and enters into time and space. Christ is God living among humanity—the ultimate break-in.

44

- Explain these points:

    —*Logos* is the Greek word for *Word*; it means the ultimate source of all human knowledge.

    —The Logos became flesh. God broke in and entered.

    —The miracle of the Incarnation is that God desires to continually break in and enter lives. Having someone in your life implies adaptation. So it is with Jesus' entry into our life.

    —Jesus "moves into" the lives of the disciples; he "breaks in" and "harasses" them for three years, and they never recover. Their lives are forever changed.

    —Jesus does not want to break into our lives just once, but constantly. May we be open and on the lookout for God's glory as it shows up in our lives and the world.

Quotation Suggestions for Slides

"Why lies he in such mean estate where ox and ass are feeding? Good Christians, fear, for sinners here the silent Word is pleading" (from "What Child Is This," words by William C. Dix, 1865).

"Our religion is clearly more sublime than any human teaching in this respect: the Christ who has appeared for us human beings represents the Logos principle in all its fullness . . ." (Justin Martyr, circa A.D. 100–165).

"The Word was first, the Word present to God, God present to the Word. The Word was God, in readiness for God from day one. . . . The Word became flesh and blood, and moved into the neighborhood. We saw the glory with our own eyes, the one-of-a-kind glory, like Father, like Son" (John 1:1-2, 14; taken from *The Message,* copyright © Eugene H. Peterson, 1993, 1994, 1995. Used by permission of NavPress Publishing Group).

Supplies

- Photos of evidence of God

- Posterboard and glue

- Muslin fabric

- Acrylic paints

- Towels and water

- Fabric markers

- Musicians or recorded music

- "Many Gifts, One Spirit"; "Here I Am, Lord"; and "Thy Word Is a Lamp" are in most hymnals.

- "Open the Eyes of My Heart" and "Every Move I Make," on *Iworship*

12 Faith Prints

The Experience: Visuals help postmodern youth make connections between their worship experiences and their lives. Visuals can also reflect the sense of community and authenticity that youth desire. Help the participants look for "Faith Prints" in their own lives and in the world. This service involves the worshipers in drama, a guided meditation, and in creating a cross with their handprints.

Environment: Any time of day; regular lighting; focus placed on the altar

Setup: Before the service, have several youth or young adults use disposable cameras to snap photos that reflect evidence of God—"Faith Prints"—in nature and in community. Give another group materials to make collages that also depict evidence of God in nature and community. Enlarge a few of the photos and display the others on posterboard. Use the photos and the collages to enhance the worship space and altar area. Create an altar cloth out of muslin (*use acrylic paint to trace everyone's handprints in the shape of a large cross during the service*). Have the participants write words (in between the handprints) reflecting the "Faith Prints" they see as evidence of their faith. Play meditative background music during the reading of Scripture, the prayer, and the offering.

Senses: *Visuals*—photos, collages, cross of handprints, drama; *sounds*—music, dramatic Scripture reading; *touch*—painting handprints in the shape of a cross and writing on the cloth

Order of Service

Call to Worship: "Many Gifts, One Spirit"

Welcome: "Fingerprints and footprints are helpful clues for investigators. Just as we leave these unique, identifying physical impressions, we are called by God to leave 'Faith Prints' on our world and in our relationships. These prints are the evidence that God is alive in our hearts, that we have been transformed."

Prayer: "God of all life, open our hearts during this time of worship. Thanks for giving us 'Faith Prints' to follow. Make us always aware of your presence. Amen."

Praise and Worship: "Open the Eyes of My Heart"
"Thy Word Is a Lamp"
(*Sing each song through twice, then have it played softly while the Scripture is read aloud.*)

Faith Scriptures: Invite three readers to read aloud the following verses (*with expression*) from different points in the room:

READER 1: "Don't let anyone look down on you because you are young, but set an example for the believers in speech, in life, in love, in faith and in purity" (1 Timothy 4:12, New International Version).

READER 2: "For we walk by faith, not by sight" (2 Corinthians 5:7).

READER 3: "Now faith is the assurance of things hoped for, the conviction of things not seen" (Hebrews 11:1).

READER 1: "What good is it, my brothers and sisters, if you say you have faith but do not have works? . . . faith apart from works is barren" (James 2:14, 20).

READER 2: "Live your life in a manner worthy of the gospel of Christ, so that, whether I come and see you or am absent and hear about you, I will know that you are standing firm in one spirit, striving side by side with one mind for the faith of the gospel" (Philippians 1:27).

READER 3: "But as for you . . . pursue righteousness, godliness, faith, love, endurance, gentleness" (1 Timothy 6:11).

READER 1: "The fruit of the spirit is love, joy, peace, patience, kindness, generosity, faithfulness, gentleness, and self-control" (Galatians 5:22).

READER 2: "For we have heard of your faith in Christ Jesus and of the love that you have for all the saints" (Colossians 1:4).

READER 3: "Fight the good fight of the faith; take hold of the eternal life, to which you were called" (1 Timothy 6:12).

ALL: "Keep alert, stand firm in your faith, be courageous, be strong. Let all that you do be done in love" (1 Corinthians 16:13-14).

(*The music softly fades as the Scripture reading ends.*)

Drama: "Faith Prints Anonymous" (See pages 49–50.)

Response to the Message: "Every Move I Make"

Prayer Time: "We have faith because of the witness of God. We have observed or experienced God through 'Faith Prints'—in other persons, through creation and the world around us, through the church and the word of God, and through experiences of the heart. Now let's pray in a time of meditation: Relax, open your hearts, and be aware of Christ's presence with us; for where two or more gather in God's name, God has promised to be with us."

(*During each pause in the following prayer, allow time for silence and meditation.*)

"To begin our time of prayer, I invite you to name in your heart those who have left 'Faith Prints' on your life—persons who encouraged and taught you faith, who lived their faith through acts of forgiveness and love. (*pause*) Remember times when you have felt God's presence through creation—a beautiful sunset, a majestic mountain, the crash of the ocean's waves, a walk through the woods, sunlight as it filtered through a tree, or a clear night when the stars shown brightly. (*pause*) Recall verses of Scripture that offered you insight, encouragement, or guidance. (*pause*) Bring to mind the melody of a song, the words to a poem, or a work of art that reminded you that life was good and worth living. (*pause*) Do you have memories of Christian fellowship on retreats, in worship, on mission trips, sitting with a friend when you felt the presence of the Holy Spirit binding you together in Christ's love? (*pause*) Have you experienced forgiveness from others? from God? (*pause*) Have you had an experience of the heart? Have you felt God's spirit at work within you? (*pause*) God's gift of faith is for everyone; but you must accept the gift. (*pause*) Spend these closing moments of silence opening your heart to the spirit of God. (*pause*) Allow God's presence to transform you from within." (*Allow a few minutes of silence, then close with the following:*)

"Strengthen our faith, Lord. Fill us with your Spirit. May our lives reflect you, your light, your beauty, your peace. Help us to leave our 'Faith Prints.' Amen."

Offering: Hand out slips of paper. Say: "Faith without works is dead. If someone were looking for evidence of your faith, what would he or she find? As an offering to God, write on your slip of paper a 'Faith Print' you will commit to making. For example, you may need to extend forgiveness to someone or to yourself. You may need to work on more loving relationships with your family or friends. You might decide on an act of service and outreach to pursue. Whatever is in your heart, write it down to be offered up to God (but don't sign the paper)."

(*Invite the youth to take their papers and leave them on the altar table and make a handprint on the cloth [forming a cross] as a sign of commitment.*)

Closing Music   "Here I Am, Lord"

Benediction (*recited in unison*):

> **"Teach us, good Lord,**
>
> > **to serve you as you deserve;**
> >
> > **to give and not to count the cost;**
> >
> > **to fight and not to heed the wounds;**
> >
> > **to toil and not to seek for rest;**
> >
> > **to labor and not to ask for any reward,**
> >
> > **except that of knowing that we do your will;**
> >
> > **through Jesus Christ our Lord. Amen."**

("Prayer of Ignatius of Loyola")

Faith Prints Anonymous

(Readers should sit in a circle or facing Nathan, as if in a support group.)

NATHAN: Welcome to tonight's meeting of Faith Prints Anonymous, a support group for those who show evidence of the Christian faith. I'm Nathan, and I'll be your facilitator for tonight's meeting. Who wants to go first?

LAURA: Hi. My name is Laura. (*Everyone says, "Hi, Laura."*) I had a really scary experience this week . . . it's difficult to share . . . I was walking down the hall at school feeling kind of down, and I caught myself humming "Amazing Grace." And that's not the worst of it. I actually felt better; and I must have smiled or something, because someone asked me—"Hey, what are you so happy about?" Do any of you know what it feels like to get caught? (*Several persons raise their hands.*)

NATHAN: We've all been caught before, every single one of us. We know what it feels like. Hang in there, Laura.

AUSTIN: Hi. My name is Austin. (*Everyone says, "Hi, Austin."*) My youth group goes to a nursing home each week to visit with the residents. You feel a lot of peer pressure to go; you can't really be part of the group unless you participate. I was uncomfortable at first. I mean, what do you say to an eighty-year-old in a wheelchair?—"How's it going?" He's going nowhere. Well, now I never miss a week. I am becoming somewhat of a "pro" at bingo!

NATHAN: It's really amazing where faith can lead you, places you would never picture yourself going. We've been there, Austin.

LIZ: Hi. My name is Liz. (*Everyone says, "Hi, Liz."*) It all started for me about six months ago. This really good friend, someone I really admired and trusted, invited me to participate in an ongoing Bible study group with her. At first I told her I just wasn't interested, and then I made up excuses for why I couldn't go. Eventually she got to me; she just wouldn't let up, and I . . . I caved. I attended that first Bible study session, and I've been going every week since. I can't stop; it has become an important part of my life.

NATHAN: It's hard to stop, Liz. Easy does it.

CATRIONA: Hi. My name is Catriona. (*Everyone says, "Hi, Catriona."*) It began innocently enough. I mean I was brought up in the church. I was baptized, confirmed, all the usual stuff. I went to Sunday school and youth group. I suppose it was a gradual thing, but one day I realized I should teach Sunday school. It's not like I just teach Sunday school, I mean I TEACH SUNDAY SCHOOL. It's been going on now for two years. I study my lesson plan and read the Bible background material, I pray for each member of the class, I write notes if they miss a Sunday, and I send them birthday cards. I love singing the Jesus songs with these little kids. Craft time is a real high for me—and we're not sniffing the glue! I realized one day that I really cared about these kids, even the difficult ones like Jamey who belches just to get laughs and Emma who cries all the time and Mary who sneaks out the door when I'm not looking. I mean I really love them, unconditionally. (*She starts to cry.*) I'm sorry. I'm afraid I'll be doing this for years. I don't think I can stop.

FROM WORSHIP FEAST: 50 COMPLETE MULTISENSORY WORSHIP SERVICES FOR YOUTH. © 2003 by Abingdon Press.

NATHAN: One day at a time. Remember, one day at a time.

MEGAN: Hi. My name is Megan. (*Everyone says, "Hi, Megan."*) OK, this is hard. I don't like to talk about it, but maybe my story will help someone else. Prayer is a private thing for me. It's something I don't share with others. I'd be horrified if someone ever asked me to lead a group in prayer. I'm telling you this so that you will understand the significance of what happened. Last week, when I was at an amusement park with my friends, we decided to ride the roller coaster. We were at the top and about to drop, when I started to pray—I mean, OUT LOUD prayer. I used to just close my eyes and scream, but all I could do was pray! In front of my friends! The worst thing is, I pray now even when I'm not afraid!

NATHAN: It's OK, Megan, it's OK. It's just one step on a long journey. Thank you for sharing tonight. We appreciate your honesty. It was from the heart. Remember that change doesn't happen overnight; it takes a lifetime. But it happens with each step we take, one step at a time. Let's repeat our prayer together:

EVERYONE: Lord, grant me the serenity to accept the things I cannot change, the courage to change the things I can, and the wisdom to know the difference. Amen. (Adapted from "The Serenity Prayer" [author unknown].)

From WORSHIP FEAST: 50 COMPLETE MULTISENSORY WORSHIP SERVICES FOR YOUTH. © 2003 by Abingdon Press.

13 Interior Changes With Exterior Impact

The Experience: This teaching service will encourage youth to let the inward changes God is making in their lives spill into their outward actions. Invite the participants to celebrate Holy Communion as a symbol of both their changed hearts and their embrace of outward holiness. Be prepared to scroll pictures that represent a lived faith, to worship around an altar table, and to have a time of commitment.

Environment: mostly candlelit room; scrolling images that capture outward expressions of faith (for instance, pictures of a mission trip, friends hugging, a group praying, and so on); worship music playing

Setup: Have chairs or pillows set in a semicircle around the altar table. Decorate the altar with fabric, candles, and different kinds of bread and juice. Leave some candles unlit so the youth can come forward to light them during the Welcome. Position the band behind the semicircle, or incorporate them into the semicircle. If possible set up two different screens: one for scrolling images, one for words of music and Scriptures.

Senses: *Visuals*—candlelight, scrolling images, Communion elements; *sounds*—music, dramatic reading of Scripture, silence; *smells*—scent of candles burning; *touch*—Communion elements; *tastes*—bread and juice

Supplies

- Candles and matches
- Communion elements
- Pictures of expressions of faith
- Band or instrument-alists
- "Veni Sancte Spiritus" and "Lord, I Lift Your Name on High," in *The Faith We Sing* (cross only edition—ISBN: 0687049040)
- Free chord charts for "Give Us Clean Hands," found at *charliehall.com*
- "You Are My King," at *verticallife.com*

Order of Service

Welcome: "Greetings in the name of our Lord Jesus Christ who lives within us and calls us to live as he lived on earth. [Band begins playing music.] Prepare your hearts for worship as you come and light a candle." [Everyone lights candles; singing begins.]

Praise and Worship: "Give Us Clean Hands"

Scripture Reading: Acts 10:1-48 (*Read dramatically from* The Message.)

The Message: (See *"Teaching Points,"* on page 52.)

The Response: "Veni Sancte Spiritus" ("Holy Spirit, Come to Us" [Taizé])

Holy Communion: (*As you prepare for Communion, talk about God changing us from the inside out.*)

Silence

Community Prayers: (*Have a time of spoken popcorn-style prayer.*)

Praise and Worship: "Lord, I Lift Your Name on High"
"You Are My King"
"Give Us Clean Hands"

Blessing and Greeting One Another

Teaching Points

- "The circumcised believers . . . were *astounded* that the gift of the Holy Spirit had been poured out *even on the Gentiles*" (Acts 10:45; italics added).

- Following God wasn't about external things anymore—doing or not doing the "right" thing, having or wearing certain physical marks, eating certain foods, hanging with the godly crowd—it was about being transformed on the inside by the Holy Spirit and life springing from that transformation.

- When an earthquake occurs in California, it is because a change has occurred beneath the crust of the earth and energy is released by the moving of tectonic plates. In Hawaii a volcano erupts and spews hot magma forth from the core of the earth. Something occurs on the interior, and this event affects the exterior.

- Too often we focus on changing our outsides, instead of letting the Spirit take hold of us on the inside and transform the way we live. Exterior changes without interior transformation cause us to think in a legalistic way about our faith—if we do this and don't do that, then we'll be "OK" with God. Instead we ought to allow God's truth to come and fill us with the knowledge and empowerment to live as Christ lived. The exterior impact of an interior change is a life marked by the teachings of Christ. In this way we are not caught up in do's and don'ts, but rather are enveloped in faithful responses to the work of the Holy Spirit. Interior changes lead to a true external impact in life.

- Peter knew a lot about external changes; he was a good Jewish man who grew up in that tradition. He was sure that one had to be circumcised to be in God's favor. His surprising experience caused him to recognize that God places a greater value on internal changes, which we experience only by the work of the Holy Spirit.

Beyond a Lame Faith

The Experience: Help youth put shoes on their faith. This service will encourage the participants to avoid becoming stuck in one stage of faith and to instead grow in their Christian walk. Pray as a community for a thriving faith that causes others to praise God. Have an artist from among your group paint an expression of thriving faith throughout the worship service. After the message ask the artist to tell about his or her work and what it says about the topic of the service.

Environment: informal; intriguing altar decorations; praise music playing prior to the service; artist's area

Setup: Place chairs or rugs in a semicircle around an altar table. Lean some crutches up against the altar and have some shoes scattered on and around the table. Have the musicians set up behind the semicircle. Invite the artist to paint at an easel next to the altar.

Senses: *Visuals*—shoes and crutches on altar, painting; *sounds*—music, silence;

Supplies

- Crutches
- Extra shoes
- An artist with his or her supplies
- "Hands and Feet," on Audio Adrenaline's CD *Hit Parade*
- "Enough," on Passion's *Our Love Is Loud* CD

Order of Service

Greeting: "As we begin our worship, come to the altar and remove your shoes. Leave them on or around the altar table as we pray that God will put shoes on our faith."

Praise and Worship: "Hands and Feet" and "Enough"

Scripture Reading: Acts 3:1-10 (*Peter heals a crippled beggar.*)

The Message: (See *"Teaching Points,"* below.)

Committing to Walk: (*Play some music during a time of silent prayer. Invite those who feel led to pray at the altar and put their shoes back on as a sign of their commitment to an active faith.*)

Closing Song "Hands and Feet"

Blessing: "In the name of Jesus, get up and walk. Walk with a faith that causes others to praise God!"

Teaching Points

- The man in the story was physically unable to move, but we can also find ourselves lame in our faith.
- Our faith can become stale when we try to function on our own. Christ has called us to grow in our faith and not get stuck in one spot.
- Sometimes our faith is lame because we sponge off our parents, our church, or others in order to feel like we have strong faith, when, instead, our faith comes from God.
- Sometimes instead of seeking deeper faith we waste time seeking useless things.
- The lame man wanted silver or gold, but was offered Jesus. Which do you choose?

53

Offerings

Supplies

- Candles and matches, incense, pictures for scrolling images, instrumental-ists for music, paper and pens

- "Come, Now Is the Time to Worship," on *Iworship*

- "Praise You," in *The Faith We Sing* (cross only edition— ISBN: 0687049040)

- "Take My Life, and Let It Be," in most hymnals

The Experience: Challenge the youth to embrace a deeper level of sacrifice and offer themselves fully to God. Through a message, praise and worship, silence, and Holy Communion, the participants will encounter God and have an opportunity to answer God's call to sacrifice.

Environment: candlelit room; scrolling images; meditative music playing

Setup: Sit on chairs or rugs around an altar table. Place the Communion elements on the altar along with some burning incense. Have the music leaders sit among the participants and provide a screen if possible for the words to the music and the Scripture passage. During the message show images of offering and sacrifice.

Senses: *Visuals*—projected pictures, offering basket; *sounds*—music; *smells*—candles and incense burning; *touch*—writing an offering, movement to song; *tastes*—bread and juice

Order of Service

Greeting: "We worship today by offering ourselves to God. Come, let us worship!"

Praise and Worship: "Come, Now Is the Time to Worship" and "Praise You"

Scripture Reading: Romans 12:1-8 (*no condemnation*)

The Message: "Offerings" (See *"Teaching Points,"* below.)

Holy Communion: (*Emphasize Christ's ultimate sacrifice as a way to consider the sacrifice to which Christ calls us.*)

Silence and Prayer: "Lord, we want to give you all we have; but we're afraid of what that really means. Show us how to trust you as much as Abraham did. Teach us that kind of obedience. Fill our hearts with love for you that we might give our lives to you as your Son gave his life for us. Amen."

Hymn of Commitment: "Take My Life, and Let It Be"

(*As the song is sung, have the youth kneel around the altar table and pray about their offerings to God. Repeat the music as the worshipers pray. Encourage them to raise their hands when the song says "Take my hands" and stand when the song says "Take my feet." When the youth are finished, proceed with the Blessing.*)

Blessing: "Go now and give yourself to God. Trust in God and don't hold back."

Teaching Points

- Talk about incense in worship as an offering to God.
- The Communion elements symbolize Christ's offering and the opportunity for us to submit an offering to God.
- God instructs us to give an offering—to sacrifice our lives for God's sake.
- We usually think of offerings in terms of money in the plate, but God calls us to give ourselves up for God's use. What is your offering? your aroma to God?

16 Seeing Is Believing

The Experience: Have a healing experience for your youth by inviting them to let water wash over their eyes. Help them feel the touch of Christ opening their eyes to his goodness. The participants will hear the Scripture in a time of meditation and share God's healing with all in the worshiping community.

Environment: candlelit room; chant or some other meditative-type music playing in the background

Setup: Have the participants sit in a "horseshoe" formation in a candlelit room. Place these items on a small table in the center of the worship space: candles, a pair of sunglasses, a basin filled with water, a towel. Give each person a small candle to hold.

Senses: *Visuals*—candles, sunglasses, basin, video; *sounds*—music, repeated readings, splashing water; *smells*—scents from burning candles; *touch*—water

Supplies

- Candles and matches
- Sunglasses
- A basin of water
- A towel
- Small candles for each person
- Recorded meditative music or instrumentalists
- *At First Sight* video
- "My Sacrifice," on *Weathered* CD, by Creed
- "Open the Eyes of My Heart," on *Iworship*

Order of Service

Opening Prayer: (*The worship leader lights his or her candle and names a personal prayer request. Then the leader lights the person's candle to his or her right and extinguishes his or her own candle. The next person follows suit and the process happens all around the semicircle. When all have named a prayer request, the leader says an opening prayer. Set aside the extinguished candles.*)

Opening Song: "Sanctuary"

The Visual: (*Show a clip from the 1999 movie* At First Sight. *Find the scene where Val Kilmer has had surgery on his eyes and can now see things for the first time. Make sure that you have a public performance license to show movies on home video; call Christian Video Licensing International at 888-771-CVLI.*)

Hearing the Word of God: (Have the participants close their eyes, relax and clear their minds, and begin to center their thoughts on God.)

- Invite the worshipers to listen closely to the reading of the Scripture and listen for words, phrases, or images that stand out for them.
- Read aloud John 9:1-11, 25 (*a man receives sight*), followed by a moment of silence.
- Now ask the youth to imagine being the blind person whom Jesus approaches.
- Again read aloud John 9:1-11, 25, followed by a moment of silence.
- As the youth are in a meditative state, ask them to consider where in their own lives they are in need of healing. Remain in silence and prayer. After a moment explain to the worshipers that they are invited to respond to the Word by participating in an eye-washing ritual.

55

The Response:

(As the washing begins, play in the background "My Sacrifice," by Creed.)

- "Come to the altar in pairs. Just as Christ healed the person's physical blindness in the Scripture, we too can experience God's healing in our own lives.

- "As you come with your partner, dip your hands into the basin one at a time, touch the closed eyes of your partner and say, "Lord, bring healing; bring peace; bring true sight.

- "When all have come, say a prayer for healing that God would open wide the eyes of your hearts."

Closing Song:

"Open the Eyes of My Heart"

Benediction: Join hands and close with the Lord's Prayer.

17 Road Trips

The Experience: Get the youth thinking about where God is calling them. Hold this worship service on a large sheet of cloth that features a map of the Holy Land. If you have a talented artist in your group, invite him or her to draw a big outline of the Holy Land (any Bible map can serve as a reference for this outline). The specifics are not as important as the look of a map. As the participants experience the story of Abraham, they will be challenged to listen for God's voice leading them on their faith road.

Environment: candlelit room, the feeling of walking onto the "holy land," nighttime sound effects playing

Setup: Spread out the sheet or sheets containing the outline of the map (you may need to tape several sheets together with fabric tape to achieve a big-enough floor covering. Try to have everyone sitting on the map. Set the altar table in the center of the sheet so that the youth are scattered around it. Have several unlit candles on the altar that youth will light during the Greeting. Have the band sitting among the rest of the group. Play sound effects of nighttime noises that might sound like the wilderness at night (for instance, crickets chirping, owls hooting, leaves rustling).

Senses: *Visuals*—map for floor covering; *sounds*—sound effects of night noises, music; *smells*—scent of candles burning; *touch*—feel of sitting on the floor covering, writing on the sheet

Supplies

- Candles and matches

- Several sheets of fabric or paper—featuring a map outline of the Holy Land

- Sound effects recording

- Markers for each person

- "I See You," on *Songs 2* CD, by Rich Mullins

Order of Service

Greeting: "Welcome to the Holy Land. We are here to worship, to linger in God's land, and to hear God's voice tell us where to go. Come and worship. [*Band begins playing music.*] Light a candle to represent your presence with us here, and let us sing."

Opening Song: "I See You"

Scripture Reading: Genesis 12:1-5a (*Call of Abram*)

The Message: "Road Trip" (See "*Teaching Points,*" on page 58.)

Guided Meditation: "Close your eyes and make yourself comfortable. Stretch out so that each of you has enough personal space. Take a deep breath in and out. Listen to the sounds of living things on the road. Imagine that you are Abram when he hears the voice of God telling him to go. How do you respond to God? (*pause*) You gather your belongings and your family and you set out on the road ahead. What are your feelings? (*pause*) God has promised to bless you. How does that make you feel? (*pause*) Now think about your life today. When have you heard God telling you to do something? (*pause*) What is hard to obey? Why? (*pause*) Imagine that God is calling to you right now. Picture yourself gathering your

57

things and setting out on the road. Listen to the sounds of the road. (*pause*) Where are you going? To what destination has God called you? (*pause*)

Will you go? Now take a minute and listen to God. Have a conversation with your Heavenly Father about where God is leading you. (*pause*) How will you respond? Take another deep breath and open your eyes. In your space on the floor, write any thoughts you have about your experience on the road." (*Allow a few minutes of silence.*)

Faith Journey Testimonies: (*Invite the participants to talk about where they are on their journeys and about the destinations to which they believe God is calling them.*)

Closing Song: "I See You"

Teaching Points

- Road trips are exciting, challenging, and fun, if you have an adventurous streak.

- What does God say to Abram? Leave! Go!

- This journey would be not only uncomfortable, but also filled with uncertainty.

- What does Abram do? (*Read aloud again Genesis 12:4-5a.*)

- He went! Note that he didn't go alone—he went in community.

- God is calling us to step out in faith, to step out of our comfort zones and into faith.

- So what does that mean for us as a community and as individuals? (*Invite responses.*)

- What does it mean for us to step out of the normal and into the uncertain?

- Will you go? Let's go—because we can go on the road together.

18 Prone to Wander

The Experience: Help the youth understand that it is human nature to think we can do all things on our own—that we don't need God sometimes. Encourage them to give their lives fully to God, but also to accept grace when they find themselves wandering away.

Environment: candlelit room, scrolling images of various roads, chant music playing

Setup: Have pillows or rugs in a semicircle facing the projection screens with the altar in the center. Position the band off to the side of the semicircle.

Senses: *Visuals*—liturgical dancer(s); *sounds*—music; *touch*—wandering in wonder

Supplies

- Candles and matches
- Images of roads and wilderness
- Chant music
- Pillows or rugs
- Liturgical dancers
- Both hymns can be found in most hymnals

Order of Service

Opening Hymn: "Come, Thou Fount of Every Blessing" (*first two stanzas*)

Scripture: Romans 7:14-25 (*inner conflict*)

Response: "Lead Me, Lord"

An Act of Praise: (*Invite one or more liturgical dancers to portray our tendency to wander away from God.*)

The Message: "Prone to Wander" (See "*Teaching Points,*" below.))

Response to the Word: "Come, Thou Fount of Every Blessing" (*third stanza*) (*As you sing the response, invite the youth to wander around the room as they make the song their prayer. When the song ends, have them join hands for the Blessing.*)

Blessing: (*Stand and join hands.*) "When we don't hear God's voice on the road, it may not be because God is not there. Though prone to wander, stay close to the Lord. Go and be obedient, even when you cannot hear. Hold the Word of God in your heart. Amen."

Teaching Points

- Paul struggles with adhering to God's laws in the same way that all of us wander away from what we know we should be doing.
- This account in Romans is an honest depiction of human failings. We are on the narrow road together.
- We sang "Come, Thou Fount of Every Blessing," which includes these words: "Let thy goodness, like a fetter, bind my wandering heart to thee. Prone to wander. . . ."
- Believe in this God who seals our hearts together and walks with us on the road.
- Thank God that Jesus Christ will rescue us when we go astray.

59

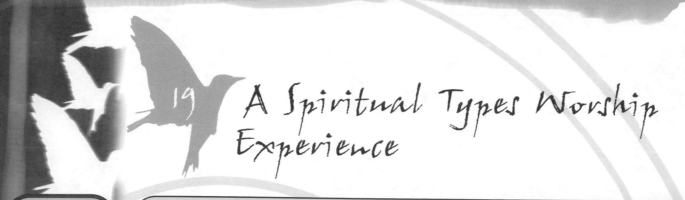

A Spiritual Types Worship Experience

19

Supplies

- Bible and pen for each person

- Photocopies of the Spiritual Types Inventory (page 65)

- Pictures of Jesus in the Temple or preaching; pictures of Jesus with children, laughing, or with the disciples,

- Pictures of Jesus praying alone, overturning the tables in the Temple (video of this scene)

- *Godspell* DVD

- Hymnals, CDs, or songbooks for your selected songs

The Experience: Interest in spiritual types—categories of spiritual experience and preference—is growing among youth and young adults. One popular new Christian website—*www.methodx.net*—is designed around four spiritual types. Corinne Ware wrote a book called *Discover Your Spiritual Type: A Guide to Individual and Congregational Growth* (Alban Institute, Înc.; ISBN: 1566991498; 1995) that helps congregations understand the role spiritual types have in their ministries. These resources are excellent tools for helping people discover the ways that they best relate to God and the directions in which they still need to grow.

Few of us would fall into just one spiritual-type category. Indeed, a healthy and whole spirituality strives for some balance among the types. Jesus is our model in this regard. Within the Gospels, we find different stories showing Jesus in all four categories—Sage, Lover, Mystic, and Prophet. In this worship service the youth will have a chance to identify one of the four as their primary spiritual type, and they will get a taste of the ways in which Jesus fits all four categories.

This service would be a great retreat or workshop. It will probably be too long to fit into your regular worship time. Consider making it a series, or retreat.

Environment: open and bright; focused on community building by getting to know one another better

Setup: Make and hang four simple banners with one of the four types printed on each banner. Put the banners in separate corners of the room if you have a flexible seating arrangement. Make four large signs to use during the service that say: Mind, Heart, Soul, Strength. Each section of the printed service that deals with one of the spiritual types contains choices for developing that part of the service. Aim for about twelve to fourteen minutes for each of the four types (assuming an hour-long service). To become familiar with the four spiritual types explore *www.methodx.net*. Sit in a circle and have a Bible and pen for each worshiper.

Senses: *Visuals*—handouts; *sounds*—music, Scripture, silence; *touch*—quizzes

Order of Service

Opening Songs: (*Sing a few of your favorite worship songs.*)

Greeting: "How many of you have ever taken a test to see what your 'type' is—like a personality test or a test that describes what kind of job would fit you best? What are some of those tests you have taken? [for example: Myers Briggs, tests in popular magazines] Did you know that there's even a test to discover your spiritual type? I have copies of one right here. All the instructions you need are on the page, including how to score the test. You will have a few minutes to take the test."

60

Distribute copies of the Spiritual Types Inventory (pages 65–67) and pens. Give everyone about ten minutes to take and score the test.

Say: "Notice which quadrant of the circle on page 67 of your handout contains the most marks or spokes. I will let you know what each quadrant represents. Label the quadrants since we didn't do that for you. The Quadrant A folks are 'sages.' Everyone in Quadrant B is a 'lover.' If most of your responses are in Quadrant C, you're a 'mystic.' And if you found yourself with mostly Quadrant D answers, you're a 'prophet.' These types may not mean a lot to you right now, but basically they represent different ways people experience God and grow in their faith. During our worship today, you will learn more about your type as we look at the life of Jesus and the ways in which his faith was deep and multidimensional."

Scripture: Mark 12:28-31 (*the greatest commandment*)

Sage

Scripture: Any portion of Matthew 5, 6, or 7
                                        (*The Sermon on the Mount*)

- Show pictures of Jesus teaching in the Temple, delivering the Sermon on the Mount, and so on.
- Have a storyteller memorize and tell a large part of the Sermon on the Mount or some parables.
- Music ideas: Sing an old hymn (for instance, "A Mighty Fortress Is Our God").

Teaching Points

- Sages are "mind" people. (*Put up the "Mind" sign*.).
- Sages like for faith to make sense, for their beliefs to hold together.
- From an early age, Jesus studied the Scriptures with passion and enthusiasm. He recognized that a critical part of faith development involves a commitment to study and research.
- Jesus was called "Rabbi" (teacher) by many people. His parables have such depth that one can peel away layers like an onion to get at their true meaning.
- For sages, some explanations of God and of faith just don't make sense. For example, sages may have trouble with someone who says that a child's accidental death was God's will, or that "demon-possession" is the reason for a person's psychological illness. Sages ask deep questions that should draw all of us deeper into the Bible.
- Sages often challenge us to consider different interpretations of Scripture based on the latest research and scholarship. Some non-sages might find these interpretations threatening, but for sages they are a quest for truth.
- Tell a story about a "sage" in your congregation searching for a connection between faith and understanding.

Discussion Questions

- In what ways do you see Jesus as a sage?
- In what ways do you seek to make your own faith make sense?

Lover

Scripture: John 11:1-44 (*Jesus heals Lazarus.*)

- Show pictures of Jesus with children, Jesus laughing, Jesus with his disciples and friends.
- Show the clip from *Godspell* where Jesus calls his disciples and then paints their faces. (*Make sure that you have a public performance license to show movies on home video; call Christian Video Licensing International at 888-771-CVLI.*)
- Music ideas: "Jesus, Lover of My Soul" or "Love Song for a Savior," by Jars of Clay

Teaching Points

- Lovers are "heart" people. (*Hold up the "Heart" sign.*)
- Jesus as "lover" isn't about sexual or romantic love but about caring, compassion, and a deep respect for and interest in others.
- The shortest verse of the Bible, "Jesus wept," (John 11:35 NIV) is actually an important part of this story. It reminds us that Jesus experienced deep emotions. He had loved Lazarus deeply. During his life, Jesus wept, laughed, told stories late at night by the fire, and appreciated the simple things of life. He lived from his heart.
- Jesus obviously had tremendous people skills. He had many disciples and friends who followed him from place to place.
- To live from the heart is to risk being vulnerable, to open ourselves to disappointment and heartache. It's the opposite of being aloof and detached and even "cold-hearted." Jesus risked loving others.
- Tell a story or two about a member of your congregation who lives from the heart—a retired person who volunteers at the hospice center, a teenager who assists persons with disabilities at a church camp, and so on. If possible, send some youth out with a video camera to record the members in action.

Discussion Questions

- Why is the "lover" form of Christianity seemingly the most common these days?
- What stories tell you that Jesus was a person of emotion and heart?
- What would the church be like if few or none of us were "lovers"?

Mystic

Scripture: Luke 5:16 (*Jesus withdraws to pray.*)

- Show pictures of Jesus praying or meditating alone, or Jesus in the wilderness.
- Music ideas: Sing one or two Taizé chants (see *www.taize.fr*).
- Spend three to five minutes, or longer, in complete silence.

62

Teaching Points

- Mystics are "soul" people. (*Display the "Soul" sign.*)
- As someone has said, Jesus came apart so he didn't come apart. Often in the Gospels he goes somewhere to be by himself for prayer and renewal. He knew that if he didn't refill his own cup he wouldn't have anything to offer others.
- A mystic has the ability to experience wonder and a connection to all life. Such a person can tune out the noise of the world to tune in to God's voice.
- If everything in our lives has to make sense, to be proved scientifically, or be understood, then we are indeed "poor in spirit" and are ultimately undermining our faith.
- Albert Einstein, the great physicist, said something to the effect of: the mystical is the most beautiful feeling we can have. To believe the unbelievable is the foundation of religion.
- To cultivate the mystic within you, you must develop the disciplines of silence and solitude. Take a walk in the woods. Listen carefully to well-crafted music. Catch snowflakes on your tongue. Study a bug. Write in a journal and periodically go back to read what you wrote.
- Tell a story of a time of wonder and awe in your own life.

Discussion Questions

- What are some other stories that tell you that Jesus was a mystic?
- When have you had a mystical experience of God?

Prophet

Scripture: Mark 11:15-19 (*Jesus turns the tables.*)

- Show pictures of Jesus overturning the tables in the Temple, persons serving others.
- Show a video clip of Jesus overturning the tables in the Temple (most movies about the life of Jesus include this scene).
- Invite a volunteer or employee associated with a homeless shelter or other social service agency to speak briefly about his or her work.
- Music Ideas: "O Young and Fearless Prophet"; "Ubi Caritas (*Live in charity*)" [Taizé]

Teaching Points

- Prophets are "strength" people. (*Display the "Strength" sign.*)
- The word *prophet* is often misunderstood. The biblical prophets didn't predict the future like Nostradamus or a fortune teller. Instead, prophets spoke to individuals or communities as messengers of God or as mediators of God's spirit. They often spoke words of indictment, pointing out the sin of the wealthy and powerful and warning Israel of the consequences of abandoning their relationship with God. They called people to restore their relationships with God and with one another.
- Prophets spoke out of their intense experiences of God. They had tremendous compassion for poor and oppressed and a deep sense of God's anger at those who oppressed others. As a result, they were usually unpopular.

- Many of Jesus' actions and stories were prophetic ones—healing those who were untouchable and unclean, criticizing the Pharisees, hanging out with prostitutes and tax collectors, challenging common interpretations of Scripture, telling parables about the kingdom of God.
- For us to claim the prophet within, we need to do, be, and tell:
  —*Do* the will of God by acting to bring about justice in the world.
  —*Be* the kind of people we call others to be.
  —*Tell* the world about God's intention for humanity.

Discussion Questions

- In what ways have you felt like a prophet?
- Who are the prophets among us today?

Celebrating Spirituality: Give youth a chance to talk about their experience and the discovery of their spiritual types. Open the floor for testimonies, celebrations, questions, or other comments. Affirm the growth that has taken place and challenge the youth to find ways to live out their new-found spiritual type. Ask:

- How can you use your spiritual discovery for God?
- To what are you being called in light of your learnings today?

Closing Song: "Spirit of the Living God"

Closing Activity and Benediction: Ask each participant to move to the sign that represents his or her dominant spiritual type.

Say: "I encourage you to check out *www.methodx.net* sometime this week. You will find there a community of people in addition to the people you're standing next to who experience God in ways that are similar to yours.

"Now go into the world as sages, lovers, mystics, and prophets; and seek the Lord in the ways that are most meaningful for you. At the same time, never forget that Jesus directed us to love God with all our heart, and all our soul, and all our mind, and all our strength. Amen."

Spiritual Types Inventory

For each multiple-choice item below, circle the answer that best fits you. In the cases where two choices have equal weight for you, circle both answers. When you have finished, follow the instructions for scoring your test (*don't read them in advance*).

1. **The ideal class assignment is a**
   A. research paper
   B. group presentation
   C. journaling activity
   D. community service project

2. **If you did the grocery shopping for your family, which would you consider first?**
   A. calories and nutrition
   B. what everyone likes best
   C. taste and flavor
   D. what organic foods you could get and/or the companies' social profile

3. **If all four of these TV shows were on simultaneously, which would you watch?**
   A. a documentary on a topic you're interested in
   B. a comedy like Friends
   C. a nature program with very little commentary
   D. a news program on world peace

4. **The ideal after-school job is**
   A. one where you have to use your head and solve problems
   B. one where you regularly work with a team of people
   C. one where you work alone and can think, reflect, and listen to music
   D. one where you feel you make a real difference in the world

5. **It is easiest for you to love God with your**
   A. head
   B. heart
   C. soul
   D. strength

6. **If you were a tree, which would you be?**
   A. a big, old oak by a stream
   B. a shade-giving elm in a park
   C. a solitary evergreen on a mountain
   D. an apple tree in someone's backyard

FROM WORSHIP FEAST: 50 COMPLETE MULTISENSORY WORSHIP SERVICES FOR YOUTH. © 2003 by Abingdon Press.

7. **What kind of music lyrics do you generally prefer?**
   A. ones that make you think
   B. love songs
   C. Why does music need lyrics?
   D. ones about social issues

8. **What do you like best about school?**
   A. the intellectual challenge
   B. the opportunities for interacting with others
   C. the chance to learn more about yourself and the world
   D. discovering how you can make a difference in the world

9. **Which of these careers would you enjoy the most?**
   A. university professor
   B. recreation director on a cruise ship
   C. novelist
   D. director of a soup kitchen

10. **If you were lost in a forest, your strongest impulse would be to**
    A. study your map, the sun, or the stars
    B. yell for help
    C. sit quietly until you sensed where to go
    D. just start walking, blazing a trail if you needed to

11. **What's your favorite part of a church service?**
    A. a good sermon
    B. the music
    C. the prayer and quiet times
    D. hearing about stories of those in mission to others

12. **If you were buying a new car, what feature would you look for first?**
    A. safety and reliability
    B. color and eye appeal
    C. size (either large or small)
    D. great gas mileage

13. **Your idea of a great first date is**
    A. a well-planned night of activities and stimulating conversation
    B. shopping and a movie at the mall
    C. a quiet walk by the seashore
    D. making cookies to deliver to a homeless shelter

14. The person in front of you in the express lane at the supermarket has a cart full of groceries. You would probably
A. quickly scan the other lanes to see which would be the fastest
B. turn around and start a conversation with the person behind you
C. grab a magazine and start browsing the articles
D. tap the person on the shoulder and gently remind him or her to choose another lane

15. Which of these is your strongest quality?
A. deep thinking
B. strong emotions
C. good intuition
D. acting and doing

Scoring

For each answer, make a spoke (like a wagon wheel) in the appropriate quadrant in one of the circles below: (A = Sage, B = Lover, C = Mystic, D = Prophet).

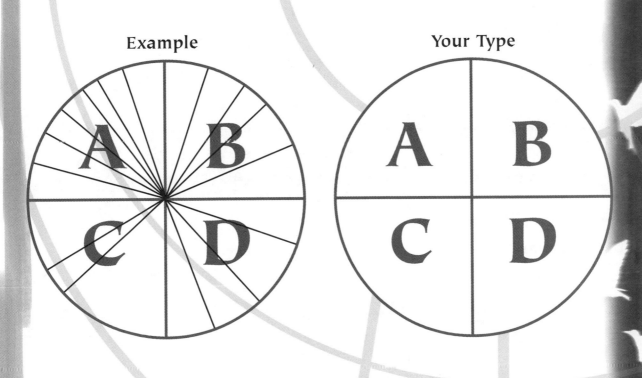

Example   Your Type

20 Taste and See

The Experience: This Holy Communion service will help the participants "taste and see that the Lord is good." By tasting freshly made, warm bread, the youth will literally taste goodness.

Environment: candlelit room, smell of baking bread, scrolling images of bread and chalices, chant music playing

Setup: Decorate the altar with a chalice and a bread machine (with bread baking in it). Set up chairs or rugs in a semicircle with the band placed behind the semicircle. If possible, have two different screens: one for scrolling images, one for words of music/Scriptures. Begin baking bread in a breadmaker before the service so that the bread will be warm for Communion.

Senses: *Visuals*—Communion elements, scrolling images, breadmaker; *sounds*—music, silence; *smells*—baking bread; *touch*—warm bread, juice; *tastes*—fresh bread and juice.

Order of Service

Greeting: "O taste and see that the Lord is good; happy are those who take refuge in him" (Psalm 34:8).

Opening Hymn: "Taste and See"

Scripture Reading: Psalm 34:1-8 (*The Lord is good.*) (*Read in unison.*)

The Message: "Taste and See" (See *"Teaching Points,"* below.)

Holy Communion: (*Prepare for Communion by singing "Holy, Holy, Holy Lord" from the Iona Community of Scotland.*)

Silence and Prayer

Praise and Worship: "Jesus, Draw Me Close"

Blessing: "Experience the Lord's goodness all the days of your life. Amen."

Teaching Points

- Consider the meals we "taste and see." In the same way that our bodies crave food, our souls beg for God's goodness, which we can taste and see all around us. We can experience God's goodness.

- The text says, "Taste and see." It does not say, "Learn about God and see; it is about experiencing God in a hands-on way.

- We come to the Table of our Lord for Communion and we are invited to "taste and see."

- God's goodness is greater than we can fully know. We can, however, get a taste of it, a glimpse. Let us experience the goodness of the Lord.

- Fill up on God as we celebrate God's goodness together.

Worship Feast: 50 Complete Multisensory Services for Youth

21 Beauty From Brokenness

The Experience: God can turn any situation into good for God's glory. Help the youth find a place in the restorative work of God in the world. A mosaic wall hanging and charcoal prayers created by the worshipers will serve as visible signs of beauty coming out of brokenness. These activities will remind the participants that God calls us to communicate God's beauty to a broken world. Celebrate Holy Communion as the ultimate act of God's restorative love.

Environment: Candlelit worship space; meditative music playing; creativity in the air

Setup: Sit in a circle with the altar in the middle. Have candles, a cross, a broken loaf of bread, a chalice of juice, and a small cup (for each worshiper) on the altar table. Decorate the altar with several bowls of broken glass that will be used for a mosaic.

Senses: *Visuals*—Communion elements, broken glass; *sounds*—music, glass being turned into beauty, silence; *touch*—gluing glass to metal, drawing prayers with charcoal; *tastes*—bread and juice

Supplies

- A plain metal sheet for making a mosaic

- Several different colors of glass pieces (found in craft stores and not too sharp)

- Glue, paper, and charcoal for drawing

- "It's Just Like You," by Waterdeep on *Open the Eyes of My Heart 2* CD

Order of Service

Opening Song: (*Sing several of your favorite worship songs.*)

Greeting: "When we are broken, God promises to restore us. When we are hurting, we can find joy in God's love. When we feel ugly, we can experience God's beauty. Look at the faces around you. Say a prayer of celebration for your community by exchanging this greeting with one another: 'You are God's and you are beautiful.' "

Scripture Reading: Isaiah 61:1-7 (*God restores and delivers.*)

The Response: "It's Just Like You" (*Play or have someone sing this song by Waterdeep.*)

The Message: "Beauty From Brokenness" (See *"Teaching Points,"* on page 70.)

Making Beauty From Brokenness

After the message, invite the youth to make a mosaic wall hanging by gluing broken pieces of glass to a metal square. When they have finished the mosaic, explain that charcoal will represent ashes as they take some charcoal and paper and draw their prayer for God to turn their ashes into beauty, their sadness into gladness. When they have finished their drawings, instruct the participants to bring their prayers to the altar and leave them there. They are then invited to experience God's restoring power through the beauty of Holy Communion. Have each person tear off a piece of bread from the loaf, and take a small cup and pour his or her own juice into the cup for the time of silence and Communion.

69

Silence and Prayer

The Response: "Amazing Grace"

The Benediction: "The Spirit of the Lord be upon you and anoint you to bring good news to the poor. Proclaim God's love and beauty to the world and seek justice for the oppressed. Amen."

Teaching Points

- The Scripture lesson teaches us that God is a restorer and deliverer.

- God calls us to be bring good news to the oppressed and heal the brokenhearted.

- We have probably all experienced brokenness in our lives. How did we experience God's healing? Who proclaimed good news to you when you needed it most?

- God makes beauty from ashes, gladness from sadness, strength from weakness. How could you be a part of that transformation for others? In other words, how might you bring good news to those who need it?

- Read verses 3b-4 again. We are the ones who will build up from ruins, repair ruined situations, and work for healing in devastations. What will we do?

22 The Many Faces of God

The Experience: God is mysterious and wonderfully diverse. In God's mystery and "bigness," all can come to God as they are. This service will help the worshipers experience the mystery and wonder of being a child of God. Through *lectio divina* and a quiet walk to find mystery, the participants will be transformed in their faith.

Environment: Set the mood of worship with a combination of darkness and candles. Play some chant music as the participants arrive.

Setup: Place several candles on a low altar table. Set a small electric water fountain, some pictures of Jesus, a Bible, and other symbols of faith on the altar. Have the youth gather into a circle and remain silent until the music is finished.

Senses: *Visuals*—gathered symbols; *sounds*—music, silence, running water; *touch*—walking to find symbols of God's mystery

Supplies

- Bibles

- "Mysterious Ways," on *Achtung, Baby* CD, by U2

Order of Service

Greeting:

LEADER:	In this place,
	In this moment,
	God is present.
ALL:	**A mystery of love**
LEADER:	Around us, within us,
	Above us, beneath us,
	God is present.
ALL:	**A mystery of love**

Praise and Worship:

(Choose two of your group's favorite praise choruses and sing them together.)

Lectio Divina Reading:

1 Samuel 3:1-10 *(Samuel's call)*

Instruct the participants to close their eyes and focus on their breathing. Tell them that you are going to read a passage three times.

71

1st Reading: *Say:* "As I read the passage this first time, I want you to just listen to the text. Don't try to think about it, just simply listen to it." (*Read aloud the text.*)

Silence

2nd Reading: *Say:* "As I read the passage this time, I want you to listen for a word or phrase that jumps out at you. Once you have your word or phrase, simply repeat it to yourself several times. (*Read the text again.*)

Silence

3rd Reading: *Say:* "As I read the passage this time, I want you to picture God. What does God look like to you? What does God's voice sound like? How might you express who God is? (*Read the text again.*)

Silence

Prayer Walk: After you have finished the reading, invite the participants to reflect on the images they thought of during the reading. Then give the youth ten minutes to comb the church, inside and out, to find something that symbolizes the mystery of God to them. Tell them to make sure not to go into offices. Remind the youth to remember where they found the objects so that they can return them later.

When the time is up, call everyone back together. Have the youth sit in a circle, holding their objects.

Play "Mysterious Ways," by U2. As the song plays, pass the symbolic objects around the circle, allowing the youth to touch and feel the symbols of faith. Continue to pass the objects around the circle until the song ends.

Read aloud the Scripture passage once again. Invite volunteers to talk about the objects they chose and how each object represents God's mystery and wonder.

Closing Song: (*Sing a favorite hymn or praise song.*)

(*Remember to have the youth return the objects to their original locations.*)

23 Worship With Wesley

The Experience: This service attempts to capture the richness and sacredness of ancient texts and so that youth can experience them in today's world (an exercise in "ancient-future"). John Wesley was a reformer in the 1700s who challenged the Church of England to have a heart-experience of God. He was sure that being Christian meant more than simply knowing Christian things—that following Jesus was about actively living out one's faith. Wesley's theology and writings are indeed rich texts for youth to begin to explore.

Environment: Foster a sense of bringing old writings into today's world for youth. Worship in your regular worship space and bring Wesley to life for your group.

Setup: Sit in a circle. Set an open Bible in the center of the circle. Provide a hymnal and a Bible for each worshiper.

Senses: *Visuals*—Bibles, the faces of the gathered community; *sounds*—ancient texts, hymns

Supplies

- Bible for each participant

- Hymnal for each participant (Note: Most of the hymns used in this service can be found in any hymnal, but all can be found in *The United Methodist Hymnal*.)

Order of Service

Greeting: "John Wesley desperately wanted the Church of England to have a heart-experience of God, instead of just head-knowledge about God. As you worship today, you will be reciting and reflecting upon some of Wesley's writings from the 1700s. He wanted us to praise God with our whole lives—from our singing to our friendships to how we live out our faith. Many denominations were born out of his passion—Methodists, Nazarenes, Pentecostals, and others. Let's join our hearts to his passion as we worship."

Opening Song: "O for a Thousand Tongues to Sing" (*In between stanzas, have different volunteers read aloud Wesley's "Directions for Singing" from John Wesley's* Select Hymns, *1761. Directions IV, V, and VII are quoted below.*)

Before the first stanza, read aloud IV: "Sing lustily and with a good courage. Beware of singing as if you were half dead, or half asleep; but lift up your voice with strength. Be no more afraid of your voice now, nor more ashamed of its being heard, than when you sung the songs of Satan."

Before the third stanza, read aloud V: "Sing modestly. Do not bawl, so as to be heard above or distinct from the rest of the congregation, that you may not destroy the harmony; but strive to unite your voices together, so as to make one clear melodious sound."

Before the seventh stanza, read aloud VII: "Above all sing spiritually. Have an eye to God in every word you sing. Aim at pleasing [God] more than yourself, or any other creature. In order to do this attend strictly to the sense of what you sing, and see that your heart is not

73

carried away with the sound, but offered to God continually; so shall your singing be such as the Lord will approve here, and reward you when he cometh in the clouds of heaven."

Community Greeting: Use the words John Wesley spoke at the very end of his life. Turn to those near you and say, "Best of all, God is with us!"

Prayer (*read in unison*): "I am no longer my own, but yours. Put me to what you will, rank me with whom you will. Put me to doing, put me to suffering. Let me be employed for you or laid aside for you, exalted for you or brought low for you. Let me be full, let me be empty. Let me have all things, let me have nothing. I freely and heartily yield all things to your pleasure and disposal. And now, O glorious and blessed God, Father, Son, and Holy Spirit, you are mine, and I am yours. So be it. And the covenant that I have made on earth, let it be ratified in heaven. Amen." (*Adapted from "A Covenant Prayer in the Wesleyan Tradition"*)

Response to Prayer: "Lead Me, Lord" (*Sing these lines: "Lead me, Lord, lead me in thy righteousness; make thy way plain before my face"; Samuel Sebastian Wesley, 1861.*)

(*Before the Scripture reading, read aloud the first and third stanzas of "Whether the Word Be Preached or Read," by Charles Wesley [italics added]:*)

"Whether the Word be preached or read, no saving benefit I gain from empty sounds or letters dead; unprofitable all and vain, unless *by faith* thy word I hear and see its heavenly character.

"If God enlighten through his Word, I shall my kind Enlightener bless; but void and naked of my Lord, what are all verbal promises? Nothing to me, till *faith divine* inspire, inspeak, and make them mine."

Scripture Reading:
Ephesians 2:1-10 (*new life*)

The Message: (*Have five different youth tell about each of the doctrines.*)

Wesley claimed that the Methodists had no novel doctrines, meaning they were not new or unique. What he termed "Our Doctrines" were the principles of all Christian churches. Hear now five primary beliefs of the church:

1. *Justification by Faith.* John Wesley felt a freedom from working for his salvation in a powerful heart transformation. Our right relationship with God—justification—is never based on our works, or earning our own way; it is a gift of grace that we accept by faith.

(*Sing the first and third stanzas of "And Can It Be That I Should Gain."*)

2. *New Birth.* Through justification by faith, our relationship with God is changed. Through new birth, we are changed. We open ourselves to God's power through Jesus Christ to transform us. We can know all about Jesus and not know Jesus. New birth is about knowing and living in Christ.

(*Sing the first and second stanzas of "O Come and Dwell in Me."*)

3. *The Witness of the Spirit.* This is a mystery. The presence of the Holy Spirit deep within assures us of our relationship with God. Wesley referred to Romans 8:16: "It is that very Spirit bearing witness with our spirit that we are children of God." Charles Wesley interpreted this concept in his great hymn "And Can It Be That I Should Gain" as "No condemnation now I dread."

(*Sing the fifth stanza from "And Can It Be That I Should Gain."*)

4. *The Declaration of the Law to Believers.* The law is used not to condemn or to justify but as a guide for believers on their journey of discipleship. The law is a call to obey Christ and make him the Lord of our lives. The example he set for us in love is the law by which we now live.

(*Sing the first stanza from "I Want a Principle Within."*)

5. *Christian Perfection.* This doctrine can be confusing. Can we be perfect? To strive for perfection is not to be neurotic or legalistic or self-righteous. It's a call to lose yourself in Christ, to be perfect in love. When we are perfect in love, we have lost our selfish preoccupation and are focused outward on others. Charles Wesley wrote the hymn "Love Divine, All Loves Excelling" that says: "lost in wonder, love, and praise." That is Christian perfection—when we forget ourselves and our desires and live in the love and wonderment of God.

(*Sing the first and fourth stanzas of "Love Divine, All Loves Excelling."*)

Offering: "In John Wesley's sermon 'The Use of Money,' he urges Christians to '*Gain all you can. . . . Save all you can. . . . Give all you can. . . .*' Early in Wesley's life, he made thirty pounds a year, about fifty dollars. He decided he needed twenty-eight pounds to live on and gave two pounds away. From then on, he lived on twenty-eight pounds and gave the rest away—no matter how much he made. In that spirit, let us give our offerings."

Call to Discipleship: "This is a reading from John Wesley's conversion at Aldersgate: 'In the evening, I went very unwillingly to a society in Aldersgate Street, where one was reading Luther's preface to the Epistle to the Romans. About a quarter before nine, while he was describing the change which God works in the heart through faith in Christ, I felt my heart strangely warmed. I felt I did trust in Christ, Christ alone for salvation; and an assurance was given me that He had taken away *my* sins, even *mine*, and saved *me* from the law of sin and death.'

"Can you recall a time when you felt your 'heart strangely warmed'? If not, is this something you desire? Are you willing to grow in faith and like Wesley, live your faith? In these next few minutes of silence, examine your heart as you pray."

Closing Hymn: "Blest Be the Dear Uniting Love"

Benediction: The inscription inside John Wesley's Bible consists of two Latin words: *Vive hodie* (*VEE-vay ho-DEE-ah*), which means "live today." So go . . . and "live today!"

A Stop on the Journey

24

Supplies

- Candles, incense, and matches

- Bibles in different translations

- Readers for the different languages

- Taizé songs found in *Songs From Taizé* (ISBN: 2850401285)

The Experience: Worship in the style of the Taizé community as you meet for singing and silence. Taizé is a village in France where an ecumenical order of brothers have dedicated their lives to reconciliation, hospitality, and prayer. Young people from around the world spend time there to pray and talk with the brothers. Help the youth experience a Taizé prayer service by singing prayers and waiting in silence.

Environment: candlelight, incense burning

Setup: Form a cross out of pillar candles in the center of your worship space. Invite the youth to sit on the floor wherever they want, in whatever posture they desire. Have songbooks available, or project the songs onto a screen. Prior to the service talk to the participants about the kind of service you'll be having so they are prepared for the freedom and silence. Spend some time at the Taizé website (*www.taize.fr*) getting to know the community. Part of the richness of Taizé prayer services is the use of different languages. If possible have the youth read the Scripture lessons in different languages, and encourage them to sing the songs in various languages. (In the Taizé songbooks, lyrics are printed in several languages.) Sing each song over and over again until the Spirit leads you to the next song. Let a holy rhythm take over your worship space.

Senses: *Visuals*—cross made of candles; *sounds*—repetitive singing, silence; *smell*—burning incense; *touch*—posture

Order of Service

Opening Prayers: "Bless the Lord My Soul

     "Lord Jesus Christ"

     "Come and Fill Our Hearts With Your Peace"

Scripture Lesson: Hebrews 10:19-25 (*Persevering together*)

Preparing for Silence: "Wait for the Lord"

Silent Prayer: (*Prior to the service, determine how long you will remain in silence. Ten minutes is appropriate. The youth may need a few minutes to get situated and comfortable in the silence, but give them time to experience waiting on God.*)

Closing Prayer: "Let Your Servant Now Go in Peace"

Remember Your Baptism

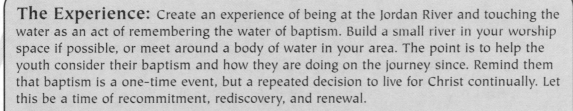

The Experience: Create an experience of being at the Jordan River and touching the water as an act of remembering the water of baptism. Build a small river in your worship space if possible, or meet around a body of water in your area. The point is to help the youth consider their baptism and how they are doing on the journey since. Remind them that baptism is a one-time event, but a repeated decision to live for Christ continually. Let this be a time of recommitment, rediscovery, and renewal.

Environment: Sounds of running or splashing water

Setup: If possible, create a "river" in your worship space by laying down a few tarps. Lift the sides of the tarps and set bricks or other heavy objects on each side of the edge to make a pool. Make the pool as long as is possible in your space. Set rocks of varying sizes on the tarp and fill it with water. You will need a wet-vac to tear down the "river" afterward. Have towels ready to clean up any spills and wipe hands and feet. Play sound effects of running water or have a fountain running throughout the service.

Senses: *Visuals*—river; *sounds*—running-water sound effects, splashing water; *touch*—the water

Supplies

- Several tarps
- Bricks or stones
- Water
- Sound effects of running water or an electric water fountain
- Wet/dry vacuum
- Towels
- Bibles
- "Down to the River to Pray," on *O Brother, Where Art Thou?*
- "Let the River Flow," on *Iworship*
- "Peace Like a River," in most songbooks, including *The Faith We Sing* (cross only edition— ISBN: 0687049040)

Order of Service

Opening: "We are here to remember our baptisms. Some of us were baptized as infants, others as children, and some may not be baptized yet. Today we come together to dip our hands and feet in the water and to make a recommitment or a new commitment to living in Christ. Come to the water."

Praise and Worship: "Down to the River to Pray"
 "Let the River Flow"

Scripture Reading: John 7:37-38 (*rivers of living water*)
 Isaiah 35:5-7 (*streams in the desert*)

Prayer: "God, let your holy water splash your love into our lives. Renew in us the passion for spreading your good news. Let us be like streams in a dry and deserted world. Make rivers of Living Water rush out of our hearts into the world. Amen."

Remembering: Explain that you will have a time of renewal and commitment. Invite the youth to walk in the water, or sit with their feet in the water and be in prayer. Encourage them to feel the presence of God as they touch the water. Have an extended period of silence as they linger in prayer. Play soft music in the background.

Closing Song: "Peace Like a River"

Blessing: "Leave here renewed by the waters of baptism. Amen."

26 A Service of Contemplation

The Experience: In this service the participants will examine several different Scripture readings and be asked a question upon which to reflect in silence. Help the youth connect their thoughts and actions to the Scripture reading and then consider how they are living out the gospel.

Environment: The service should feel like a Bible study set in a worship context.

Setup: Scatter rugs or pillows around the room. Make a slide for each Scripture verse and question and project the slides onto a screen. Have paper and pens for each worshiper who chooses to write answers in a journal. Play praise music in the background and invite volunteers to read aloud each Scripture once before the silence. Observe silence in between every Scripture passage.

Senses: *Visuals*—projected Scriptures and questions; *sounds*—spoken Scriptures, silence, music; *touch*—posture, journaling

Order of Service

Call to Contemplation: " 'Whoever wants to be first must be last of all and servant of all' (Mark 9:35b). Come before God, meditate on Scripture, and offer silent prayers of confession and thanksgiving."

The Scriptures: Luke 22:24-27 (*Do you consider yourself the greatest?*)
Galatians 5:13-15 (*Do you say, "I love my neighbor" then complain about everyone?*)
Galatians 1:10 (*Do you try to please people, or serve Christ?*)

Sung Response: "Open the Eyes of My Heart, Lord"

The Scriptures: 2 Timothy 2:23-24 (*Do you get caught up in stupid arguments?*)
John 12:23-24; 26a (*Are you following Jesus?*)

Sung Response: "Open the Eyes of My Heart, Lord"

Blessing: Read in unison Philippians 2:5-11 (*imitating Christ*). Then say, "You have thought in your mind and heart about your faith. Now go to live Christ's love to the world, serving others and glorifying God. Amen."

27 An Agape Feast

Supplies

- Table decorations
- Nice dishes and napkins
- Candles, matches, and centerpieces
- Enough pastries for all the participants to have their fill
- Water and another beverage
- Recordings of classical music
- "In the Lord I'll Be Ever Thankful," in *The Faith We Sing* (cross only edition— ISBN: 0687049040)

The Experience: Build community among your group members by recognizing the sacredness of sharing meals together, and by experiencing an ancient tradition in the church. Love (*agape*) feasts started from the Moravian tradition and have seen a revival in many Christian denominations today. An agape service is conducted with praise, prayer, thanksgiving, Scripture, and song. This service is different from Communion in that it is a less formal and more spontaneous ritual that calls a gathering to community. Testimonies or witnesses to the Scriptures are a primary focus.

Environment: candlelit room, set up for a banquet

Setup: Have long tables connected together so that everyone has a seat around the table. Decorate the tables with tablecloths, candles, centerpieces, and so forth. Set trays of various pastries down the middle of the table and have water and another beverage in pitchers. Use cloth napkins and nice dishes to make the meal extra special. Play classical music softly in the background. Invite several participants to prepare to give a witness to the Scripture.

Senses: *Visuals*—the banquet spread; *sounds*—soft music, Scripture, testimonies; *smells*—pastries and candles; *touch*—table, food; *tastes*—pastries, drinks

Order of Service

Prayers: "Let us turn our hearts toward God and be in prayer for those whom we name aloud. When you have stated your request, close with, 'Lord, in your mercy' and we will join in saying, 'Hear our prayer.' Now let us pray."

Close the intercessions with this prayer:

> "Father of earth and heaven,
>   Thy hungry children feed,
> Thy grace be to our spirits given,
>   That true immortal bread.
> Grant us and all our race
>   In Jesus Christ to prove
> The sweetness of thy pardoning grace,
>   The manna of thy love.

(From *The Love Feast*, by Charles Wesley, copyright © 1992 by The United Methodist Publishing House)

Praise and Worship: "In the Lord I'll Be Ever Thankful" (*from Taizé*)

First Scripture Lesson: Luke 14:7-14 (*humility and hospitality*)

79

The Witness to the Scripture: (*Invite a few of the youth to talk about what they hear in the Scripture.*)

Second Scripture Lesson: Luke 14:15-24 (*the parable of the Great Dinner*)

The Witness to the Scripture: (*Invite a few of the youth to talk about what they hear in the Scripture.*)

The Passing of the Bread: (*While the pastries are passed around the table, invite volunteers to share a brief testimony.*)

The Sharing of the Loving Cup: (*Distribute the beverages around the table.*)

Personal Confession of Sin: (*Silence*)

Assurance of Pardon in Jesus: 2 Corinthians 5:15-17; 1 John 1:8-9

The Response: "In the Lord I'll Be Ever Thankful" (*from Taizé*)

Benediction: "We have shared testimonies, Scriptures, songs, bread, and Christ's love and we can be sure that we are one in Christ. As we continue feasting at God's heavenly banquet, let us love one another. Amen."

(*Stay at the table as long as your group wants to. Continue the feast over conversations about school, work, sports, faith, and so forth.*)

28 A Worship Service for Graduates

The Experience: This service gives you an opportunity to "send off" your graduates and makes the transition a special time for everyone. The group members will get to tell each graduate what he or she has meant to them as well as pray for their future.

Environment: Best held outdoors in late afternoon. Have the participants sit in a circle on the ground.

Setup: Before worship begins, give the graduates index cards and have them write names of teachers, family members, leaders, and friends who have been supportive of them during high school.

Senses: *Visuals*—outdoors, the faces of friends; *sounds*—testimonies, songs, sounds of the outdoors

Supplies

- Index cards
- *The Faith We Sing* (cross only edition— ISBN: 0687049040)
- Bibles
- Song that has been special for your group

Order of Service

The Call to Worship: Psalm 117 (*Praise the LORD*)

Opening Hymn: "In His Time"

A Prayer of Thanksgiving for Our Graduates:

Amazing God, by your wisdom we are taught the way and the truth. Bless [*call out names of graduates*] as they finish high school [*or college*] and bring to a close this part of their lives. We thank you for teachers, family, leaders, and friends who have supported them along the way. Walk with these graduates as they leave and move forward in life. Take away the stress and anxiety of not knowing what comes next. Give them insight and strength to use the gifts with which you have blessed them. Help these graduates use their gifts to serve you and further your kingdom. May they be a blessing to those around them and may they see you in all they experience. Amen.

(*Pause and allow each graduate to tell about one name written on the index cards that he or she has found to be supportive in his or her life.*)

Scripture Reading: Romans 8:31-39 (*Nothing can separate us from God.*)

Testimonies: In turn, have each graduate move to the center of the circle. The other members of the group will tell one at a time what that person has meant to them personally and what they will miss about him or her.

Prayer for Graduates Leaving the Group *(said responsively)*:

This youth group is a family,
united by faith in Jesus and our friendships around this circle.
We are all brothers and sisters;
and for a time, this youth group is our home.
Like every human family our youth group is formed and reformed over time: Members come into the group, members also leave, members are adopted into our family, and they leave our youth group for new places and new experiences. Together we have shared with one another good times and bad; we have shared joys and concerns; we have laughed and cried. As you move into a new part of your life, know that you are not alone. We will pray for you in all that you do and wherever you go.

Let us pray *(said in unison)*:

O God, our Protector,
keep and preserve our friends leaving the youth group,
in all health, and safety, both of body and soul;
through Jesus Christ. Amen.

Closing Song:

(Play a song that has been a youth group favorite and is meaningful to the seniors.)

Benediction: "[Now may] the LORD bless you and keep you; [may] the LORD make his face to shine upon you, and be gracious to you; [may] the LORD lift up his countenance upon you, and give you peace. [Amen]" (Numbers 6:24-26)

29 A "Blessing of the Youth Room" Worship Experience

The Experience: Before the service have group members bring in ideas, pictures, and colors related to how your space might look. Encourage the youth to make suggestions about how to arrange the chairs and the meeting area, how to arrange other furniture, and about what colors to paint the room. If your church is supportive, allow the youth to actually initiate the remodeling process (painting, rearranging furniture, putting up posters and pictures, and so on). The central idea is for the whole group to be involved in changing the structure of the room in order to have more ownership of it. This service is the final touch on the remodeling.

Environment: Excitement around the remodeled room; openness to visitors

Setup: One week before the room is to be blessed, announce to the group members that they are to bring to the "blessing" a "room-warming gift" that represents who they are (maybe a picture, or something from their own bedroom). As the youth arrive, they should sit in a circle with a bare worship table in the middle of the space with one small lit candle. (The participants are to bring their gifts with them.) Play some favorite CDs as background music for the service.

Senses: *Visuals*—new look for youth room; blessing gifts; *sounds*—favorite music playing, unison prayer and commitment; *smells*—candles burning; *touch*—bringing gifts to the altar; *tastes*—snacks to celebrate

Supplies

- Candles and matches

- Favorite CDs and a CD player

- Snacks and beverages

- "Lord, I Lift Your Name on High," in most songbooks, including *The Faith We Sing* (cross only edition— ISBN: 0687049040)

Order of Service

Greeting: "Jesus said: 'Listen! I am standing at the door, knocking; if you hear my voice and open the door, I will come in.' [Revelation 3:20]

"We are here to celebrate this special place. A special place that we have worked hard to make welcoming and warm and sacred. We now ask for God's blessing over this room that this may be a place of acceptance, a place where all God's children feel loved, a place of respect and encouragement, and a place where we can grow in friendship with one another and with God. We now bring praise to God for this wonderful place and we offer this space to God just as we offer ourselves as God's servants."

Unison Prayer: "Wonderful God, bless this room and come into it so that we will know all of our days that you are present among us. Help this room, and all who are here, to be a welcoming 'safe place' to both visitors and friends. In your name and that of your Son and the Holy Spirit we pray. Amen."

The Scripture Lesson: Ephesians 3:14-21 (*prayer for the readers*)

The Commitment (*said in unison*):

"In the name of the Father, the Son, and the Holy Spirit, we commit ourselves to making this room an inviting and welcoming place. We will treat all who enter as members of God's family and accept visitors as part of the group.

"Lord God, please bless our youth room and all the youth who will come here. Allow your love to rest upon us. Help us to grow in grace, knowledge, and in love. Amen."

Have everyone go around the circle one at a time and show the gift that she or he brought and tell why it is significant. Then have each participant place the gift on the altar table.

Have a love feast to celebrate the consecration of your room. Feast in God's goodness and presence with you as you call on God to lead your group.

Closing Song: "Lord, I Lift Your Name on High"

30 Building the Community of Faith

The Experience: Help the youth get an idea of what an apostolic church meeting might have felt like, in a service that helps them define what kind of community they will be. Celebrate Communion as an act of community in Christ.

Environment: Create a sense of mystery around the meeting. Meet in an unfinished basement or home to simulate the environment of the early church. Have scented candles lit all around, the smell of fresh bread lingering, and meditative music playing.

Setup: Provide chairs or rugs in a semicircle with the altar table in the center; no instruments are needed. If possible have bread, in its final stage, baking (use a bread machine appliance in the worship space; begin baking the bread one or two hours prior to the start of the service). Place juice for Communion on the altar and an empty offering plate or basket at the foot of a cross. Make available pens and slips of paper for "The Response."

Senses: *Visuals*—basement, Communion elements; *sounds*—testimonies, silence, a cappella singing; *smells*—scented candles burning, baking bread; *tastes*—freshly baked bread for Communion, juice

Supplies

- Paper and pens
- Bread machine and bread mix
- Communion elements
- Cross and candles to decorate an altar; matches
- "In the Secret" and "You Are My King" at verticallife.com
- "Shine, Jesus, Shine," in *The Faith We Sing* (cross only edition—ISBN: 0687049040)
- The Doxology, in most hymnals

Order of Service

Opening Praise and Worship: "In the Secret"
"You Are My King"

The Greeting: "Grace to you and peace from God our Father and the Lord Jesus Christ [1 Corinthians 1:3]. Turn to those around you and offer the peace of Christ."

Testimonies: (*Invite the worshipers to give their testimonies. Allow enough time for all who want to participate.*)

Praise and Worship: "Shine, Jesus, Shine"

Scripture Reading: Acts 2:37-47 (*the early church*)

The Message: "Being a Christian Community" (See "Teaching Points," on page 86.)

Holy Communion: (*Invite a volunteer to tell the story of the Last Supper and then proceed with your traditional ritual.*)

85

The Response: "What will you give to build this community? Imagine the urgency and excitement that filled the air of the early church. Imagine being there when the Holy Spirit came upon those believers. Now imagine that it's your group to whom the Holy Spirit comes. What does the Spirit call you to offer to the community? We have broken bread with generous hearts, praised God, and enjoyed the goodwill of all the people. How now will we share all things in common? Write your response to these challenges on your slips of paper; when you are ready, offer them to God by placing them in the offering plate [or basket] on the altar. If you feel led, linger at the cross. Pray in the silence. Let us pray."

Closing Prayer: (*Invite a volunteer to close in prayer.*)

Hymn: The Doxology

Blessing: "The grace of the Lord Jesus be with you. My love be with all of you in Christ Jesus" (1 Corinthians 16:23-24).

Teaching Points

- **How was the early community of faith built?**
  — By willing leaders who committed to being the church despite all efforts to stop them
  — By people who stood up for their faith and were ready to die for the gospel
  — By the power of the Holy Spirit

- **Summarize Acts 2:1-35.**
  — Coming of the Holy Spirit
  — Peter's sermon to the many
  — The first-ever "altar call"—like Thursday night at church camp

- **Play "What if . . ."**
  — What would it have been like if the leaders of the early church had never lived? Or if they had never decided to act on what God was doing? The apostles dedicated themselves to acting on God's movement in their lives.

- **Devotion to God and to community: To what else were the disciples devoted?**
  — Teaching
  — Fellowship
  — Breaking bread
  — Prayer
  — Keeping all things in "common" (shared resources)
  — They did all of this daily

- **Do we have devotion to God? If so, how do we show that devotion?**
  — Are we willing to teach, participate in fellowship, enjoy meals together, pray, and daily share our lives?
  — Are we devoted to Christ? to this Body of Christ?

31 From Here to There

The Experience: Take your group members on a walk with Jesus. Help them hear the Scripture message as it speaks to them in this worship time. On the way to the cross, the participants will travel to three "villages" around the worship space and be given a token at each destination. Finally at the cross, the group members will linger in prayer and give up the tokens they acquired on the way.

Environment: Band/Praise and Worship; Scriptures read aloud; teaching; silence; two different screens (one for scrolling images, one for words of music/Scriptures)

Setup: Place chairs or rugs in a semicircle (*instrumentalists will play from around the semicircle*). Create three stations or "villages" in the room with a table, a map, and an object representing the learning at each village. (*Station 1:* This station represents Jesus' rebuke of James and John, which conveyed that power is not the road Jesus chose. Give each worshiper a rock to take away from this station as a symbol of power. *Station 2:* Provide a pillow and a toy house (Monopoly® pieces work fine) to signify that our home is in Christ, not in a physical place. Supply a cotton ball for each worshiper to take away from this station as a symbol of softness and comfort. *Station 3:* Use a planner/calendar and a to-do list to symbolize the excuses that we make to keep from following Jesus. Have a page torn from a used date book for each worshiper to take away from this station to symbolize busyness.) Finally, arrive at the cross.

Senses: *Visuals*—Scripture stations, tokens, handouts; *sounds*—walking as a group, music; *touch*—walking, tokens, handouts

Supplies

- A rock, a cotton ball, and a used datebook page for each person

- Three tables

- Three maps

- Large rock

- Small pillow and toy house

- Calendar or planner and a to-do list

- Large cross

- "I See You," on *Songs 2* CD, by Rich Mullins

- Hymnal

Order of Service

Praise and Worship:
"I See You"
"He Leadeth Me: O Blessed Thought"

The Gospel Lesson:
Luke 9:51-62 (*A Samaritan village refuses to receive Jesus.*)

The Message: (*Invite the worshipers to get up and follow you around the worship space. First, stop at the "Samaritan village" where Jesus rebukes James and John, suggesting that power will not help them on their spiritual journey. Walk on to the next "village" where you will explain that the road might not be comfortable. Go next to the last stop before the cross where your group members will discover that their to-do lists must be surrendered in order to follow Christ. Finally, arrive at the cross where the worshipers will stop and pray and offer the symbols they have acquired along the way. Distribute the handout on page 89 and ask the youth to examine their journey through the Scripture. Invite them to draw a road of their personal journey with Jesus. When they are finished, ask for volunteers to tell about their roads. Discuss the highs and lows. Talk about the time when they have felt especially close to Jesus.*)

Praise and Worship: "I See You"

Blessing: "Give yourselves completely to Christ. Follow him closely and don't look back. Amen."

Teaching Points:

- Recall the text: Walking with Jesus must have been the ultimate road trip. And on their way to Jerusalem many people joined in.
- How do people respond to Jesus on this trip?

Station 1

- When Jesus and his disciples were unwelcome in a Samaritan village,
  — James and John want to call fire down upon the village.
  — Jesus rebukes them, saying *no to power*.

Station 2

- A man is eager to follow Jesus:
  — Jesus responds, "Foxes have holes, and birds of the air have nests; but the Son of Man has nowhere to lay his head."
  — Jesus says *no to security*.

Station 3

- Two other persons come to Jesus:
  — Jesus says, "Follow me" to the first, who replies, "First let me go and bury my father."
  — The other person proclaims a willingness to follow Jesus but asks to say goodbye to his family first.
  — Jesus replies to these legitimate requests, "Let the dead bury their own dead. . . . No one who puts a hand to the plow and looks back is fit for the kingdom of God."
  — Jesus says *no to anything that keeps us from giving ourselves completely*.

At the Cross

- What can we see when the disciples went from here to there with Jesus?
  — They were in motion. They were always on the move toward Jerusalem—toward the cross and ultimately the Resurrection.
  — Static faith was not an option.
  — They went together. They became part of the rag-tag community where everyone belonged.

88

From Here to There

Draw a road map of your journey with Jesus. Include times when members of the group have supported you. Include difficult times when you wanted an easy solution. Make your drawing a prayer of thanksgiving for your community and for the faithfulness of Christ. You may take it with you or leave it at the cross as an offering.

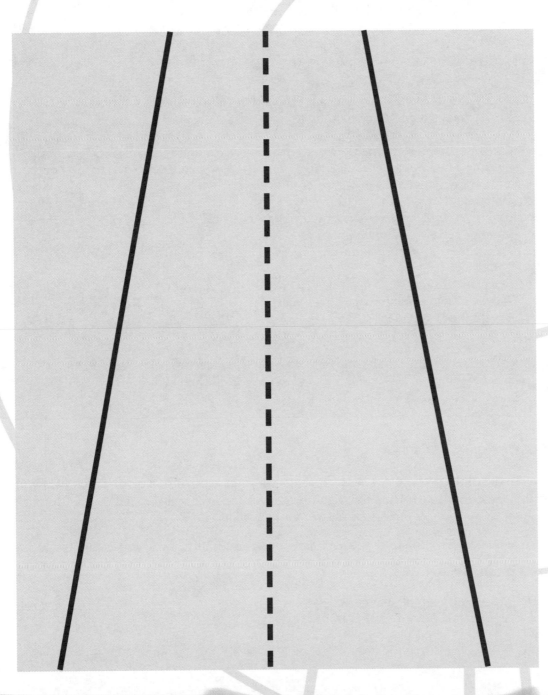

Supplies

- Three tables for meditation stations

- Pictures of leaders for justice or victims of injustice and descriptions about the leader or the victim

- Three candles and matches

- Large sheets of paper for prayer wall

- Markers and art supplies

- Current newspapers

- *Romero* video and *Gandhi* video or other videos and a VCR

- *The Battle of Los Angeles* CD, by Rage Against the Machine

- *Before These Crowded Streets* CD, Dave Matthews Band

- Hymnal

32 Just Us for Justice

The Experience: This service will take a bit of preparation and awareness. A great place to have this worship would be in an empty, stark room such as an abandoned warehouse, or a location that might symbolize justice or injustice.

Environment: Set the tone of a prayer vigil. Promote a sense of being free to wholly be in prayer.

Setup

1. Set up three meditation stations. Each station should feature a picture of this nature: of someone who stood up for justice, such as Martin Luther King, Jr., Gandhi, or Oscar Romero; or of a person or group of people who were victims of injustice, such as Matthew Shepard or refugees around the world. Have a candle burning at each station beside the picture along with a brief description of each person's connection with justice or injustice.
2. On one of the walls of the worship space, post large sheets of paper for a wall of prayer on which the youth can write prayers.
3. Supply markers and art supplies for writing on the prayer wall.
4. Provide current newspapers for sources of articles related to peace and justice issues.
5. Be ready to show film clips from the movies *Romero* and *Gandhi* or another film that shows people standing up against injustice.
6. Secure these CDs: *The Battle of Los Angeles,* by Rage Against the Machine, and *Before These Crowded Streets,* by the Dave Matthews Band.

Senses: *Visuals*—meditation stations, newspapers, videos; *sounds*—video clips, responsive reading; *touch*—walking to and experiencing each station

Order of Service

The Gathering: Hand out newspapers. Have small groups find articles that deal with social injustice. Ask each team to write a prayer related to that issue. Tell the youth that they will get a chance to use their prayers later in the worship time.

As the teams are creating their prayers, play the song "Testify" by Rage Against the Machine.

The Greeting

LEADER:	In a world where there is war,
ALL:	**We come together in peace.**
LEADER:	Where there is hate,
ALL:	**We come together in peace.**

LEADER:	Where some people die from hunger and some live in excess,
ALL:	**We come together in peace.**
LEADER:	Where God comes to us and invites us to hang out,
ALL:	**We come together in peace.**

Song of Calling: "What Does the Lord Require of You?" (*or other appropriate song*)

Prayers From the People: (*The groups present their prayers.*)

The Scripture Lesson: Micah 6:6-8 (*what God requires*)

The Message in the Movies: (*Show one or two clips from the chosen movies.*)

Response: Invite volunteers to tell something that was particularly meaningful from the movie clips.

Stations of Justice: Invite the worshipers to spend some time in prayer and meditation at each station, focusing on how God is calling them to be instruments of peace. As the youth feel moved to do so, encourage them to write or draw their own prayer or commitment statement on the "Wall of Prayer."

Play music in the background as the time spent at the stations begins. When the participants begin to move toward the prayer wall, play "Last Stop" by Dave Matthews.

Come back together for the closing prayer. Have the participants recite together "The Prayer of Saint Francis":

> Lord, make me an instrument of thy peace;
> where there is hatred, let me sow love;
> where there is injury, pardon;
> where there is doubt, faith;
> where there is despair, hope;
> where there is darkness, light;
> and where there is sadness, joy.
>
>
> O Divine Master,
> Grant that I may not so much seek
> to be consoled as to console;
> to be understood, as to understand;
> to be loved, as to love;
> for it is in giving that we receive,
> it is in pardoning that we are pardoned,
> and it is in dying that we are born to eternal life. [Amen.]
>
> (*Francis of Assisi, Italy, thirteenth century*)

91

33 Mission Trip Follow-up

Supplies

- Symbols that represent the mission-trip activities

- Paper and markers for making signs

- Items from trip to bring to the altar for the procession

- Photos and other items from trips for display purposes

- Photo turned into a coloring page for the Children's Message

- Hymnals or songbooks

The Experience: Many youth groups take part in extended mission trips during the summer or school breaks. Usually, the whole congregation has been involved in making the trip possible by participating in various fundraisers, praying for the youth, volunteering with different aspects of the trip, and so on. Here is a simple and effective service outline that can be used time and time again by the youth as they develop a worship service to inform the whole congregation about their trip.

The service assumes that the youth worked in separate crews. If your group worked together in just one or two teams, or if your group is small, simply have individuals speak rather than representatives from each group. If you don't know the hymns suggested on the following pages, choose other mission-related songs from your church's hymnal or songbook—preferably ones with multiple verses.

Environment: An atmosphere of joy and of gratitude to the community for helping the youth participate in a mission project

Setup: Around the worship space, project or display pictures and items from the trip. Also, make and hang signs with mission-oriented phrases such as "Go," "Send me," "Radical Availability," "Wash more feet," "Get your hands dirty," "Here I am, Lord," and "You are Jesus' hands and feet." Choose an item that each person in the congregation can bring to the altar at the end of the service as a symbol of his or her commitment to missions. For example, if your group repaired homes, give everyone a strip of cloth to place on a small model-house frame to symbolize blanketing the family with love. Or if the group helped lead a Bible school, give everyone an eight-inch piece of yarn to drape over a cross as a symbol of tying one's own life to the lives of those who are in need of Christ's love. You could also simply give everyone a small piece of paper on which to identify a new commitment.

Senses: *Visuals*—photos from trip and symbols to bring forward; *sounds*—stories and testimonies from trip; *touch*—carrying symbols to the altar

Order of Service

Prelude: Invite one of the participants to play a song, or have the group sing a number of the songs they learned during their trip.

Introit: Instruct the youth to process forward from the back of the sanctuary as they sing the chorus to "Sanctuary." Each person should carry something symbolic of the trip to place on the altar—a hammer, a work shirt, a lunch box, and so on. The last person could carry a simple cross made out of two-by-fours.

Call to Worship

LEADER:　　On this and every day, God gives us light and calls us to come together in the light.

PEOPLE:　　**At the dawning of a new day, we are given an opportunity for a fresh start with one another, a new chance to live in the light.**

LEADER:　　Humble yourselves and worship the Lord, so that you may be equipped for service.

PEOPLE:　　**We are called by God to a life of trust in God and compassion for God's creation.**

LEADER:　　Come today not for nuggets of wisdom but for transformation and powerful demonstrations of the way of Christ.

PEOPLE:　　**We are the salt of the earth, seasoning it with God's love. We are the light of the world, showing God's works to everyone.**

Hymn: The opening song should be a praise song used during the trip.

Prayer of Confession: Gracious God, hear the cries of your people. Come to us in the midst of our chaos and confusion and help us to see all that you have prepared for us. We confess that we often put ourselves before others and our own desires before yours. We have chosen our own limited knowledge rather than your limitless wisdom. We have been caught up in our own petty disagreements rather than the plight of the oppressed, and we fed our egos while we forgot the hungry. Stop us in our tracks, God. Show us a new road to travel. Forgive us, guide us, and help us to change. Amen.

Epistle Lesson:　　　　　　　　　　　James 1:17-27 (*doers of the Word*)

Work Crew Report/Testimony by One of the Youth

Children's Message: Many graphics programs allow one to simplify a photograph and convert it into a coloring-book drawing. Do this with a picture from the trip and make a copy for each child.

Pass around the original picture and/or an item of significance from the trip. Talk about its meaning by telling a story from the trip; also tie the picture to serving God by serving others. Give each child the coloring-book page to take home as a reminder that when we help others, we serve God.

Ministry of Music: Suggestions: Have a soloist or group sing one of these items: a song learned during the trip; a song that comes from the place, country, or culture where the youth served; a mission-related song such as "Hands and Feet" by Audio Adrenaline (on the Hit Parade CD).

Gospel Lesson:　　　　　　　　　　Luke 10:25-37 (*the good Samaritan*) or
　　　　　　　　　　　　　　　　　　　Matthew 25:31-46 (*the least of these*)

Hymn: (*first stanza only*)　　　　　(*Suggestions*)
　　　　　　　　　　　　　　　　　　　"Cuando El Pobre" ("When the Poor Ones")
　　　　　　　　　　　　　　　　　　　"As a Fire Is Meant for Burning"
　　　　　　　　　　　　　　　　　　　"Together We Serve"

Work Crew Report/Testimony by One of the Youth

Hymn: *(second stanza)*

Work Crew Report/Testimony by One of the Youth

Hymn: *(third stanza)*

Work Crew Report/Testimony by One of the Youth

Hymn: *(fourth stanza)*

Prayer: *(written by one or more of the youth)*

The Lord's Prayer

Offering: *(with songs by one or more of the youth)*

The Community Responds: Introduce the last hymn by saying: "Each of you is called by Jesus to love your neighbor as yourself. Jesus tells all of us to go out into the world to serve and make disciples of all people—not just to send someone on our behalf. You received a [*piece of fabric, yarn, a slip of paper, and so on*] as you entered the sanctuary today. We invite you to come up during our closing hymn to lay that item on the [house, cross, altar, and so on] as a symbol of the ways you will recommit yourself to be in mission to a world that is desperately in need of God's love."

Hymn: "Here I Am, Lord"

Benediction: "You are children of God and neighbors to one another. So *go*, and live as God's family. You are the church, the body of Christ. So *go*, and be the hands and feet of Christ in the world. You are the light of the world. So *go*, and may there be no doubt whose light shines through you. Amen."

Hip-Hop Praise

The Experience: Instead of cringing when you think of hip-hop music, celebrate this style of music in worship with your youth. Hip-hop is a language of popular culture. One can find songs in this category that have themes of faith, God, struggle, and so forth. Build your community by having a dance worship service. Aside from the music for the service, plan to undergird the readings and even some chant music with a rhythmic beat. Youth should leave feeling as if their music can be a thriving part of their faith.

Environment: dance club feel, achieved with strobe lights and other special effects; play some chant music that has been infused with a rhythmic beat as the youth arrive.

Setup: Secure a disco ball, black lights, or other fun lighting. Set out refreshments on a table. If possible, hire a disc jockey. Or collect favorite CDs from the group members, screen them for appropriateness, and invite a volunteer to change the CDs.

Senses: *Visuals*—dancers, lights; *sounds*—music, Scripture set to beat; *touch*—moving to music; *taste*—refreshments

Supplies

- CD player or DJ
- Chant music
- Disco ball, black lights, or other fun lighting
- Refreshments
- Your group's favorite CDs
- *Salvador* CD, by Salvador
- *Thankful* CD, by Mary Mary
- *The Rebirth of Kirk Franklin* CD
- *Talk About It* CD, by Nicole C. Mullens
- *Extreme Days* CD, by TobyMac

Order of Service

Opening: "Tonight we are going to dance and praise our God. Dancing isn't just for school parties—we can dance in worship. God gave us music as a gift; and so we are going to give our loudest, most rhythmic praise back as an offering to God. Let's worship!"

Singing:
"He Reigns (The Medley)" (by Kirk Franklin)
"Talk About It (Say So)" (by Nicole C. Mullen)
(*Invite some liturgical dancers to dance as the community sings along.*)

Reading: 2 Samuel 6:12-16 (*David dances.*) (*Have someone read this passage over a drumbeat, or write a rap using the text.*)

Response: "Dance for joy, children of God. The Lord has blessed us all! If you get hungry or thirsty, help yourself to refreshments. Let's dance like David danced!"

Dancing:
"David Danced" (by Salvador)
"Shackles (Praise You)" (by Mary Mary)
"Baby Girl" (by Nicole C. Mullen)
"Extreme Days" (by TobyMac)
(*Include other favorites of your group.*)

Closing: *When your group is "danced-out," join hands and say a closing prayer. As the participants leave, turn on the beat-infused chant music.*

95

35 The Color of Worship

Supplies

- Candles and matches

- Bread in different varieties (as well as other Communion elements)

- Images of different countries and different people

- Pillows or chairs

- Fabrics in different colors and textures

- Small drums

- *The Faith We Sing* (cross only edition— ISBN: 0687049040)

- *Iworship*

The Experience: Use this service to celebrate the diversity of the kingdom of God. God's creation is a mosaic work of art and we need not be afraid of the differences. Celebrate Communion as an act of unity in the body of Christ and as a way of affirming each person's uniqueness.

Environment: candlelit room; scrolling images of people of all races in various countries; play music from different cultures; have a few artists paint, sculpt, dance, and so forth during the service.

Setup: Arrange pillows or chairs in a semicircle around an altar table. Decorate the altar with fabrics in different colors and textures. Have a variety of breads prepared for Communion that represent different countries. For instance, spicy tea bread as a symbol of the people of Ethiopia and pita bread as a symbol of persons in the Middle East. Set the Communion elements on the table. Have the band in the rear of room. If possible, have two different screens on each side of the table: one for scrolling images, one for words of music/Scriptures. Find volunteers to read the Scripture lesson in various languages. Have artists set up near the altar.

Senses: *Visuals*—artists, altar decorations; *sounds*—multicultural music, silence; *smells*—breads; *touch*—drumming; *tastes*—variety of breads for Communion

Order of Service

Opening Song: "Heleluyan (Alleluia)" (*Traditional Muskogee [Creek] Indian*)

Prayers: Give everyone a small drum and invite a volunteer to begin drumming as he or she prays silently. After a moment, invite others to join in prayer by drumming their own beat until everyone is letting the sound of the drum beat carry their prayers to God.

Praise and Worship: "Praise, Praise, Praise the Lord!" (*Traditional Cameroon*)
"Shout to the Lord"
"Over My Head, I Hear Music in the Air" (*African American spiritual*)
"Santo, Santo, Santo" (Holy, Holy, Holy) (*Argentine folk song*)

Scripture Reading: Jonah 1–4 (*various readers, alternating in different languages if possible*)

The Message: "The Color of Worship" (*Incorporate the artists as part of the message by interviewing him or her about the piece.*)

Communion: (*Let the worshipers serve one another by passing the breads around the community. Have them say, "The body of Christ broken for you" as they pass the loaves. Then pass the cup around the semicircle for the participants to dip their bread. As the cup is passed, have the youth say to one another, "The blood of Christ shed for you."*)

Silence and Prayer

Praise and Worship:
"Better Is OneDay"
"God of Wonders"
"He's Got the Whole World in His Hands"

Blessing: "God has the whole world in God's hands. Do not be fooled into thinking you are alone in this world. You have brothers and sisters on every side of the seas. We are all God's children. Let us love one another as Christ loves us. Amen."

Teaching Points

- What is the color of worship? Brown? white? black? olive?
  —What do you think of when you try to answer that question?

- Recall the text (Jonah 4:1-3; 11). Jonah was written for the Jews. The book relates the story of the failure of a person to see, accept, and celebrate the desire God has for redemption outside the scope of what was expected. Jonah basically threw a tantrum because he believed that God was being too loving.

- Jonah didn't think God should love those Ninevites. Whom do we refer to as "those people"? Who do we think doesn't deserve God's mercy?

- God cares about all of creation (including animals) and wants all of us to be connected through God.

- What is the color of the people of God? Worshipers form a mosaic or stained glass pattern. Worship is to be multicolored, involving everyone. The colors in a mosaic don't blend, but get situated together—side by side, from all angles, different sizes and shapes—to create a masterpiece.

- This is a great theme of the Scriptures: As we focus on God's desires for community, distinctions that divide us fall away, while beauty remains.

- If there is a dominant color in the mosaic, it is the color red, representing the blood of Christ shed for the sin of the whole world. He invites us to the Table tonight. Let us come to the Lord's table fully diverse and fully in community.

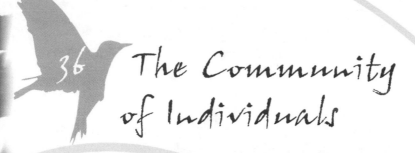

36 The Community of Individuals

Supplies

- Chairs, rugs, or pillows
- Paper
- Markers or pencils in various colors
- Simple cross
- Candles and matches
- Tape

The Experience: This service is about overcoming conflict and joining together in Christian community. As the worshipers reflect on the early church, they will be helped to grasp a sense of unity even as individuality is celebrated. Use this service prior to "The Community of Unity" (see page 100).

Environment: To increase the atmosphere of community, encourage the youth to sit next to someone they may not know very well.

Setup: Place chairs, rugs, or pillows in a semicircle. Sing without instruments. Have markers or pencils in various colors and paper laid out around the semicircle. Have a simple cross and a few candles in the center of the semicircle. Have tape ready to piece together the papers from the Response.

Senses: *Visuals*—simplicity of altar, mural; *sounds*—testimonies; *touch*—painting a mural

Order of Service

Greeting: "We are here to celebrate all the individuals who make up this community. As we worship we will learn more about one another, share our faith stories, and grow closer as a community of faith. We will begin by saying together the prayer we share in common, the Lord's Prayer."

The Lord's Prayer

Passing Christ's Peace: "Make sure to greet those here whom you may not know well. Let us celebrate Christ's peace that is abundant in our community."

Testimonies: (*Celebrate each individual in the community by giving volunteers a chance to tell what they think they bring to your community of faith.*)

Scripture Reading: Acts 6:1-7 (*the apostles are chosen*) (*Have those on one side of the room read the first three verses in unison, and the remaining youth finish the passage in unison.*)

The Message: "Building the Community"

The Response: (*Invite the worshipers to take some paper and markers and draw a picture, write a poem, or otherwise form a response to the message. Encourage the participants to think about what they bring to the community and then represent that in their creation. When everyone has finished, tape the papers together in no specific order to make a banner for your worship space. Note that the banner reflects the celebration of individuality in the midst of community. Display the banner before moving into the silent reflection time.*)

Seeking God in Silence and Prayer

Praise and Worship: *(Sing a few of your community's favorite songs to close the service.)*

Benediction: "May the Lord draw us closer to one another in love. Amen."

Teaching Points

- In the Book of Acts as well as today, the Christian church is a gathering of a group of individuals who try to function as a community. Such an effort presents a challenge, to say the least. Through the Scripture we see the reality of conflicts in the community and a responsible response to those conflicts.

- Retell the story, explaining the historical context of a growing faith community made up exclusively of Jews at first and that later included Greeks.

- The conflict in the community:
  -- The Greek widows were not being supported like the Jewish ones.
  -- Every church congregation experiences conflicts. People tend to take sides so that the situation often becomes destructive.
  -- Conflict is a reality for us; it was a reality for the early believers.

- The faithful response:
  -- Read aloud Acts 6:5-6.
  -- The Twelve gathered all the disciples and had them select seven people to be in charge of this need involving the widows in the community.
  -- Spiritual maturity and character (not spiritual gifts) were prerequisites.
  -- The community came together to solve a problem and grew from the experience of working together.

- The result:
  -- Read aloud Acts 6:7.
  -- The Word of God spread.
  -- The number of disciples increased.

The Community of Unity

Supplies

- Candles and matches
- Rugs or pillows
- Favorite songs
- Projected images of different gathered communities

The Experience: This service will help your community make a commitment to loving one another and working for unity in Christ. Help the participants celebrate diversity and call them to peace, justice, and unity for all in Christ.

Environment: Pillows or rugs, instrumentalists sitting among participants; a feeling of welcome and openness

Setup: Set rugs or pillows in a circle and have the band sit among the circle. Project the Scripture text along with scrolling images of different communities of persons. Have unlit candles on an altar table to be lit by youth as an opening.

Senses: *Visuals*—projected images; *sounds*—favorite songs, silence; *smells*—burning candles

Order of Service

Greeting: "As you center yourself for worship, light a candle to signify your presence in the community in this time. Prepare your heart to worship God."

Praise and Worship: (*Sing a few of your community's favorite songs.*)

Scripture Reading: John 17:20-24 (*one in Christ*)

The Message: "The Community of Diversity"

Silence and Prayer: (*Project the Scripture during the silence.*)

Praise and Worship: (*Sing a few more favorite songs.*)

Blessing: "Go from this place renewed by being among your community of faith. May the Lord continually remind you of the love that is always available to you and others as members of this group. Celebrate God's creation as reflected in each member of the community. Peace to you. Amen."

Greeting One Another

Teaching Points

- Last week (see page 98): We established the concept that the community of Jesus' followers is, and ought to be, a community of diversity.

- This week: We see in the Scripture lesson the need for unity.

- What kind of unity is the community of faith supposed to have?
  - -- Are we supposed to look alike? speak alike? dress alike? listen to the same music? enjoy the same food? Absolutely not.
  - -- Our unity is to consist of a unity of purpose: [Jesus said,] "*that they may all be one. As you, Father, are in me and I am in you, may they also be in us, so that the world may believe that you have sent me*" (John 17:21; emphasis added).

- The question then is, are we willing to partner (or be one) with other people (in our community of faith and beyond) so that we can have a major effect on the world for the sake of Jesus?

- Such a vision and mission involves more than a desire for friendship. Unity in Christ brings together not just friends, but brothers and sisters in Christ—from all walks of life, creeds, circumstances, and cultures. We truly are one in the Lord.

- We don't just move closer to one another on our own, but moving closer to Jesus from our separate spheres brings us closer together as believers. Saint Dorotheos of Gaza wrote that if God is the center of a circle, and the world is the circle itself, then as we move closer to God we cannot help but move closer to one another. Likewise, when we move away from God, we move away from one another. The more we love God, the more we love our neighbor. This is the community of unity we experience when we come together in the name of our Lord. Let's pray together in silence and listen for God speaking to us through the Scripture.

38 You + Me = We

Supplies

- Rugs or pillows
- Communion elements
- Art expressions from youth

The Experience: This service celebrates new participants in the group and uses worship to help the youth learn about one another. Before the worship experience invite the youth to use poetry, prose, song, drawing, and other art forms to create a special welcome for the new persons coming into the group. Youth will lead this service.

Environment: Create a feeling of welcome by sitting in a circle.

Setup: Place rugs or pillows in a circle around a small altar table. Invite the youth ahead of time to bring an artistic expression that will be a welcome to new persons.

Senses: *Visuals*—art expressions; *sounds*—storytelling in the group; *tastes*—Communion elements

Order of Service

Greeting: (*Have the youth present their items welcoming the new members of the group.*)

The Hebrew Bible Lesson: Leviticus 19:33-34 (*love strangers*) (*spoken by different readers*)

Our Traditions and Rituals: "Every group has unique traditions and rituals. For someone new it can be intimidating and awkward not to be familiar with those traditions." (*Spend some time allowing the youth to talk about and show any symbols of the special traditions of the group and what makes this group special.*)

The New Testament Lesson: Acts 2:42-47

Communion: (*Have older youth serve Communion to the new participants.*)

Closing Songs: (*Sing a few favorite praise choruses.*)

Benediction: Use your group's regular closing ritual to end the service or discuss a new closing ritual for your meetings. Numbers 6:24-26 is a popular benediction: "The Lord bless you and keep you; the Lord make his face to shine upon you, and be gracious to you; the Lord lift up his countenance upon you, and give you peace. Amen."

Advent Intrusion

The Experience: This service is about God's "intrusive" ways. Advent is a great time to experience God's holy intrusion into our lives through Jesus Christ. Use this worship service to revisit the Christmas story and observe God's activity in that event. Reflect together on the amazing ways in which God may be intruding into the participants' lives as individuals and as a community. Throughout the service have someone randomly ring a loud bell as if God is intruding into the worship time with a message.

Environment: Candlelit room decorated for Christmas; use pine and cinnamon scented candles; various scrolling images of Christmas symbols

Setup: Place chairs or rugs in a semicircle around an altar table. Have the band sit to the side of the semicircle. Set up a table for coffee, hot chocolate, snacks off to the side of the semicircle. If possible, have two different screens: one for scrolling images, one for words of music or Scriptures. Show projected images of icons of Christ, icons of Mary, the Nativity, current-day images of Christmas trees, lights, Christmas at a homeless shelter, and so on.

Senses: *Visuals*—projected images; *sounds*—Christmas songs, silence intrusive bell; *smells*—pine and cinnamon scented candles; *touch*—coffee or hot chocolate; *tastes*—coffee or hot chocolate

Supplies

- Pine and cinnamon scented candles, matches, Christmas decorations, images of Christmas, hot chocolate, coffee, and small snacks

- "Come, Thou Long Expected Jesus," in most hymnals

- "Better Is OneDay," in most songbooks, but also on Passion's *The Road to One Day* CD

- "Welcome to Our World," on *Deep Enough to Dream* CD, by Chris Rice

Order of Service

Greeting: "Christ is coming! God is coming to us in the most intrusive way—right into our world. God wants to be with us. Hallelujah! When you hear a bell ring imagine that God is intruding into your thoughts with a message. We'll pause for a moment each time to listen. Let's worship."

Praise and Worship:
"Come, Thou Long Expected Jesus"
"Better Is OneDay"

Call for Silent Confession of Sin:
"Of the Father's Love Begotten" (*followed by silence*)

Spoken Assurance of Pardon: "'For as the heavens are high above the earth, so great is his steadfast love toward those who fear him; as far as the east is from the west, so far he removes our transgressions from us' (Psalm 103:11-12). Remember this—in Jesus Christ we are all forgiven. Let us share Christ's peace with one another as we enjoy a cup of coffee or hot chocolate."

Passing of the Peace

Scripture
Luke 1:8-20, 26-38 (*Zechariah's vision, Mary's vision*)

Teaching   "Advent Intrusion" (See *"Teaching Points,"* on page 104.)

Praise and Worship: "Welcome to Our World"

Blessing: "Now may God go with you and intrude in your life. Do not be afraid. God will ask mighty things of you, but do not fear; God is with us! Amen."

Greeting One Another

Teaching Points

Project Luke 1:8-17 and read the passage in unison.
Give background on Zechariah and Elizabeth, priestly duties, and so on.
Point: In the Temple, in the context of worship, God showed up. Why was Zechariah surprised?
- God showed up and Zechariah was afraid.
- What if God showed up here tonight? Would we also be surprised? afraid?

Project Luke 1:18-20 and read the passage in unison.
Point: Zechariah questions whether God is trustworthy.
- This amazing pregnancy was predicted at a time when our modern advances in treating infertility were totally unknown.
- Following God can cause us to wonder whether our trust is well placed; we too ask the question, "How can this be?"

Project Luke 1:26-33 and read the passage in unison.
Point: God shows up in Mary's life, she learns that a unique pregnancy is in her future, and her life gets more complicated than she ever could have imagined.
- Many people have to deal with challenging news or events; for some, their life falls apart as a result.
- Mary was greatly troubled by the incredible message she received.

Project Luke 1:33-38 and read the passage in unison.
Point: Mary asks the same question as Zechariah, but the angel responds differently.
- Mary is called highly favored and blessed, but what might happen to her?
  a. She could be shunned in her community for having a child out of wedlock.
  b. Her son would probably be known as "fatherless" and ridiculed by his peers.
  c. Mary says yes, no matter what challenges and obstacles she might face.

Project an image of Christ and the words, "Don't be afraid."
- Zechariah and Elizabeth—Don't be afraid. The angel basically says to the couple, "Your son will live like a hermit and will eventually be beheaded for his prophetic role in preparing the way for the Messiah, but don't be afraid!"
- Mary—Don't be afraid. But your son will leave you and will be crucified on a cross before your very eyes.
- How is God intruding into your life?
- Has God said "Don't be afraid" but then seemingly ruined your life?
- God will ruin the plans we have for our lives and substitute God's plan instead. God longs to be in our lives. *Do not be afraid.* God is with us.

40 Preparing for a Birthday Party

The Experience: Get youth excited about and anticipating the birthday of Christ during Advent. In this service you will be making the preparations for a birthday party (read: Christmas!) Invite youth to plan the perfect birthday party around the framework below. Don't forget to emphasize that worship can be a party!

Environment: Party atmosphere, balloons, streamers, Christmas decorations ready to hang

Setup: Before the service, invite youth to bring a favorite Christmas decoration to hang in your youth room or worship space. Have on hand other decorating supplies as well. Play some Christmas music throughout the service and have Christmas-type snacks set on a table.

Senses: *Visuals*—decorations; *sounds*—Christmas music, dramatic reading; *smells*—cider and pine; *touch*—decorating the room; *taste*—Christmas-type refreshments

Supplies

- Christmas decorations
- Recorded Christmas music
- Christmas refreshments

Order of Service

Start the Party: Play some favorite recorded Christmas music and invite youth to grab some refreshments and find a seat.

Scripture Lesson: Mark 1:1-3 (*prepare the way*) (*Ask for three volunteers to read each verse. In between the verses have youth shout, "He's coming! He's coming! Our Lord is coming soon!*)

Call to Celebration: "We are here to prepare for the party that is Christmas. If you know how to party, then I invite you to celebrate Christ's coming as we decorate, fellowship, and party together. Let us hang greens, light candles, put up streamers, and praise God as we prepare for the coming of the Savior."

The Party: Enjoy a time of fellowship as you decorate the room. Listen to Christmas music, play some Christmas games, have a gift exchange, and so forth.

Singing: Sing together some favorite Christmas hymns.

Closing Prayer: "Lord we are ready for your coming. Be pleased by our preparations. Come into our hearts anew this Christmas. The party is set. Come, Lord Jesus. Amen."

Preparing the Way: An Advent Experience

Supplies

- Canned goods to be donated

- Birth announcement cards with *Jesus* printed on the cards

- Purple votive candles with a birth announcement with Jesus' name printed and tied with a ribbon

- Matches

The Experience: Spend several weeks collecting food for a local food bank. Then as a group, go to the food bank to deliver the items and spend a couple of hours sorting the food. Before you leave, have this special time of worship.

Environment: anticipation of completing an outreach project

Setup: Gather into a circle around the supplies that have been donated.

Senses: *Visuals*—donations; *sounds*—responsive reading; *touch*—traveling to food bank

Order of Service

Greeting

LEADER:	We wait for the arrival of Jesus—to come to us again.
ALL:	**What should we do while we wait?**
LEADER:	If you have two coats, give one away; do so with your food also.
ALL:	**What else should we do while we wait?**
LEADER:	Treat everyone the same—with love and respect.
ALL:	**What else should we do?**
LEADER:	Be examples of the one you wait for.
ALL:	**We will be living examples of the living Christ.**

Prayer of Thanksgiving: Have the youth think of people who have been most helpful to them in times of need throughout their lives. Go around the circle saying: "I am thankful for [*person*] because _____."

Reflection: Tell the youth that by collecting and delivering food items they have made a difference in the life of persons in need and have begun to prepare themselves and others for Christ's coming this season. Discuss the group's experience at the food pantry. Talk about preparing the way for Christ.

Scripture Reading: Read together Luke 3:1-6. (*prepare a way for Jesus*)

Closing: Give each person a small purple candle attached to a birth announcement card that has the name *Jesus* on it. Instruct the youth to put the announcement in a prominent location during Advent. They are to burn the candle every night for one minute and focus on Jesus' birth during that time.

Traveling: As you proceed to the food bank, sing together a few favorite Christmas carols.

42 Midnight on Christmas Eve

The Experience: Have a candlelight service around midnight on Christmas Eve. Start a tradition of having the midnight service with your group so that excitement builds each year. Youth will worship in candlelight and have some quiet time around the manger before the festivities of Christmas morning begin.

Environment: Candlelight

Setup: Meet in a small space so that your candles will light the space well. Gather into a circle around an empty manger. You will need a candle with a paper wax catcher (*bobeche*) for every worshiper.

Senses: *Visuals*—candles, manger; *sounds*—silence, responsive reading; *smells*—burning candles; *touch*—kneeling at the manger

Supplies

- Candles, wax catchers (*bobeches*), matches
- Empty manger

Order of Service

Greeting: "As we prepare for the light of Christ to come into the world, let us share his light around our circle." (*Light your candle and the candle of the person to your right and invite him or her to pass the light. As the light is passed, have youth say to one another, "the light of Christ be in you."*)

The Christmas Story: Prior to the service, ask for volunteers to prepare Luke 2:1-20 as a dramatic reading. Invite them to present the story at this time.

Reflection: Ask for some volunteers to talk about how they have prepared for Christmas this year. Discuss what Christmas means to each youth and how they will spread Christ's light in the world.

Praying at the Manger: Now invite youth to spend time in silent prayer around the manger. Explain that this time is just for them to spend time with Jesus. They may pray for others, for any needs they have, or simply listen for God in the silence.

Closing: "Christ is coming. Prepare a way for the Lord. When you open gifts and feast with your families tomorrow, remember why you are celebrating. Thank God for your gifts and for your family. Christ is coming! Let us sleep tonight in heavenly peace and wake tomorrow in joyful celebration. Amen."

Song for Lingering Upon: Sing "Silent Night" together. When the last stanza is sung, have the youth blow out their candles and continue humming the carol as they depart.

43 Bringing in the New Year

Supplies

- Several tealight candles and matches

- Stamped envelopes

- Paper and pens, refreshments

- All songs can be found in *The Faith We Sing* (cross only edition— ISBN: 0687049040).

The Experience: This midnight service will help bring in the New Year. Gather the group to worship, read Scripture, reflect on the past year, and pray about the year to come.

Environment: atmosphere of anticipation for the new year; reflective worship, then celebration of what is to come

Setup: Have the youth sit in a horseshoe formation. The worship space should be dimly lit, with New Year's decorations, candles, and a wooden cross in the center of the group with small tealight candles outlining it.

Senses: *Visuals*—cross, decorations; *sounds*—silence, music; *smells*—burning candles; *touch*—writing letters; *taste*—party refreshments

Order of Service

Opening: Psalm 8 (*God is sovereign*) (*various readers*)

Praise and Worship: "Awesome God"
"Humble Thyself In the Sight of the Lord"

Experience: Have the group members list on a sheet of paper the "Top 5 Most Important Things" they have experienced over the past year—both good and bad. After youth have completed the exercise, ask them to focus on their list as the Scripture is being read and to listen for what God might be saying through the Word.

Scripture Reading: Ecclesiastes 3:1-8 (*a time for everything*)

Reflection: Play some music as the youth work on their list. Have them write (on the other side of their paper) ways they can grow during this upcoming year into a better person and ways they can grow spiritually.

The Offering: Distribute stamped envelopes. Have the youth self-address the envelopes, put their sheets of paper in the envelopes, and leave their letters at the foot of the cross as an offering.

Closing: "Sing Alleluia to the Lord"

Afterward: Collect the letters after the service is over. File them away for a couple of weeks and then mail them out to the youth as a follow-up to the experience. After the worship service, play games and have snacks to celebrate the coming of the New Year.

They Have Taken My Lord . . .

Experience: This Holy Week service is designed to help participants wrestle with the times when God seems to be absent or silent. Hear Mary of Magdala's frantic cries that they had taken away her Lord. Join Mary's struggle to once again find Jesus.

Environment: Empty room with scarce lighting, set like a cave or tomb with fog machine, if possible

Setup: Create a sense of being there with Mary as she went to the tomb. Hold the service first thing in the morning, even before dawn if your youth are up to it. If you have access to a fog machine, using it would help create the feeling of early morning. Burn spicy-scented incense to represent the burial spices that Mary would use to prepare Jesus' body. Place an empty table in the center of the worship space and gather in a circle around it. Play sound effects of morning sounds (birds chirping, leaves rustling, and so forth.)

Senses: *Visuals*—fog, empty table; *sounds*—sound effects, music; *smells*—incense

Supplies

- Fog machine
- spicy-scented incense
- Sound effects of morning
- "Salvation," on Passion's *The Road to OneDay* CD
- "Calling Out Your Name," on *Songs* CD, by Rich Mullins
- "Your Love, Oh Lord," on *Offerings* CD, by Third Day
- "Shout to the Lord," in *The Faith We Sing* (cross only edition— ISBN: 0687049040)

Order of Service

Greeting: "Good morning, or not so good! They have taken our Lord. Let us go with Mary as we tell others that he is gone. Let us wait for Jesus to show himself to us!'"

Praise and Worship: "Salvation"

Scripture Reading: John 20:1-18

Sung Call for Repentance: "Calling Out Your Name"

Silence and Corporate Confession of Sin: *(led by individual in the community)*

> Merciful God, we have been calling out your name this morning.
> We confess our sins and ask for your mercy.
> We have not loved you with a pure heart,
> nor have we loved our neighbors as ourselves.
> We have not done justice,
> loved kindness,
> nor walked humbly with you, our God.
>
> Have mercy on us, O God.
>
> In your great compassion,
> cleanse us from sin.
> Create in us clean hearts, O God,
> and renew a right spirit within us.

109

Do not cast us away from your presence
or take your Holy Spirit from us.
Restore to us the joy of your salvation
and sustain us with your Spirit.

For we ask in the name of Jesus Christ our Lord. Amen.

Sung Assurance of Pardon: "Your Love, Oh Lord"

Passing of Christ's Peace

The Message: "They Have Taken My Lord"

Praise and Worship: "Shout to the Lord"

Blessing: "We have seen the Lord. Go and proclaim to all who would hear, 'I have seen the Lord!

Teaching Points

- They have taken away my Lord. . .
  - ___ Numbers of people who used to go to church now no longer find church meaningful. They might be saying, "They have taken away my Lord, and I do not know where they have laid him."
  - ___ Many friends used to have a thriving relationship with Jesus but now their lifestyle seems to contradict their faith. They might be saying, "They have taken away my Lord, and I do not know where they have laid him."
  - ___ The girl who was abused as she grew up might now be saying, "They have taken away my Lord, and I do not know where they have laid him."
  - ___ We heard a similar story in the Scriptures tonight: Mary from Magdala is confused. Jesus is not where she last left him. She laments, "They have taken away my Lord, and I do not know where they have laid him."

- Life is dynamic:
  - ___ It changes in dramatic and subtle ways all the time.
  - ___ Even though our lives change as we grow up, our faith often remains immature. Like Mary, we are left confused and puzzled: "They have taken away my Lord, and I do not know where they have laid him."

- Take note of this fact: Mary twice voices the lament that they have taken away her Lord and she doesn't know where to find him.
  - ___ According to the Scripture, God raised Jesus from the dead.
  - ___ Mary did not have all the information, but when she saw Jesus again, she knew for certain that she had seen her Lord.

- The question for us is, Who took away our Lord?
  - ___ Maybe it was us . . .
  - ___ Maybe it was the cruelty of others . . .
  - ___ Maybe it is our lack of information or patience for answers from God. . .

- Observe Mary:
  ___ She runs to tell the disciples, then they leave confused as well.
  ___ Mary waits.
  ___ Mary weeps.

- When have you felt like Mary? Confused and helpless, like God is nowhere to be found. In what ways have you been surprised by God being there all along, and in more amazing ways than you could have imagined?

- Stir up our hearts, O God. Open our spirits to an awe-filled realization of who you are. Put a cry so deep inside us that we cannot hide the words we need to speak; we just weep and cry out to you. "And Jesus was standing nearby!"

111

Great Expectations

Supplies

- Communion elements, rugs or pillows

- "What Wondrous Love Is This?" in most hymnals

- "You Are My King" and "I Could Sing of Your Love Forever," at verticallife.com

- "Better Is OneDay," on Passion's *The Road to OneDay* CD

The Experience: This service features the following themes: the Cross, the Passion of our Lord, and Holy Communion. Youth will hear the Scriptures read dramatically and be challenged to consider their expectations of God.

Environment: Darkened room, a few candles lit

Setup: Sit on rugs or pillows in a semicircle around an altar table. Prior to the service, invite three readers to practice and present the interpretive reading of the Scriptures on pages 114–115. Set unlit candles on the altar table that youth will light as the first act of worship. Have a loaf of bread and a cup of juice on the altar.

Senses: *Visuals*—Communion elements; *sounds*—interpretive reading, music; *smells*—burning candles; *taste*—bread and juice.

Order of Service

Opening: "As you come to light a candle to mark your presence in worship, think about the expectations you have for God. Expect amazing things from God as we worship. Come, light your candle."

Praise and Worship: "What Wondrous Love Is This?"

Scripture Reading: Interpretive reading of Mark 11:1-10; Luke 22:7-20; Luke 23:33-38, 44-46 [*the passion of Christ*] performed by three readers) (See page 114.)

Praise and Worship: "You Are My King (Amazing Love)"

The Message: "Great Expectations"

Holy Communion: (*Explain that the Lord's Supper is an unexpected gift of Christ.*)

Silent Prayer

Praise and Worship: "Better Is OneDay"
"I Could Sing of Your Love Forever"

Blessing and Greeting: "Go, expecting God to do marvelous things. Amen."

Teaching Points

- *What we observe and experience in life is often different from our expectations.* The three texts read tonight speak of differing expectations.

  - Consider Jesus' triumphal entry:
    - ___ After years of tense Roman occupation, the people welcome Jesus as a King.
    - ___ The crowds quote Psalm 118; they shout "Hosanna!" (*Save!*).
    - ___ This event has all the makings of a reestablishment of the golden age of the Kingdom under David.
    - ___ The disciples must have felt elated: they believed they were on the inside of a powerful revolution.
    - ___ But what did the disciples actually get? A meal where Jesus offers them his body and blood, and his crucifixion. What were they expecting?

  - Are we any different?
    - ___ We like big things and more of everything we want.
    - ___ And so we come to Jesus, nailed on a cross, and say, "Thanks—this is good, and I appreciate it, really. Now . . . can I have a new car? a new boyfriend/girlfriend, job?" The list is endless.
    - ___ We often ignore what God has done and offered because we expect more.

  - The apostle Paul also experienced a longing for more (2 Corinthians 12:1-9).
    - ___ He has a vision of heaven, receives a thorn in his flesh, and pleads with God to remove it.
    - ___ God's response (the one Paul probably wanted)? "Sure, Paul, I was just joking about that thorn. In fact, let me set you up with a villa on the Mediterranean coast with some tanned young women to feed you grapes while you compose most of what will be called the New Testament."
    - ___ God's actual response: "My grace is sufficient for you."
    - ___ Paul expectations are turned upside down—power is in weakness when he is in Christ.

  - Whether our expectations are met or turned away, God's grace is sufficient.
    - ___ At the very least, Jesus offers us (1) his death on a cross for our sin as well as the sins of the whole world and (2) this community meal where he is present.
    - ___ The question is: Are these amazing gifts enough for us? Are they enough for you? What are your expectations from this life of faith?

Dramatic Scripture Reading

Readers should read through their parts prior to the worship service. The reading is based on the passion of Christ. Listeners are pulled in and out of the familiar story experiencing it as if they are there witnessing the events.

Reader 1: (*matter-of-factly*) As they approached Jerusalem and came to Bethpage and Bethany at the Mount of Olives, Jesus sent two of his disciples, saying to them, "Go to the village ahead of you, and just as you enter it, you will find a colt tied there, which no one has ever ridden. Untie it and bring it here. If anyone asks you, 'Why are you doing this?' tell him, 'The Lord needs it and will send it back here shortly.' " They went and found a colt outside in the street, tied at a doorway. As they untied it, some people standing there asked, "What are you doing, untying that colt?" They answered as Jesus had told them to, and the people let them go.

Reader 2: Then came the day of Unleavened Bread on which the Passover lamb had to be sacrificed. Jesus sent Peter and John, saying, "Go and make preparations for us to eat the Passover." . . . "Where do you want us to prepare for it?" they asked. He replied,

Reader 3: "As you enter the city, a man carrying a jar of water will meet you. Follow him to the house that he enters, and say to the owner of the house, 'The Teacher asks: Where is the guest room, where I may eat the Passover with my disciples?' He will show you a large upper room, all furnished. Make preparations there." They left and found things just as Jesus had told them. So they prepared the Passover.

Reader 1: (*sadly*) When they came to the place called the Skull, there they crucified him, along with the criminals—one on his right, the other on his left. Jesus said, "Father, forgive them, for they do not know what they are doing." And they divided up his clothes by casting lots.

Reader 2: When they brought the colt to Jesus and threw their cloaks over it, he sat on it. Many people spread their cloaks on the road, while others spread branches they had cut in the fields. Those who went ahead and those who followed shouted, "Hosanna!" "Blessed is he who comes in the name of the Lord!" "Blessed is the coming kingdom of our father David!" "Hosanna in the highest!"

Reader 3: When the hour came, Jesus and his apostles reclined at the table. And he said to them, "I have eagerly desired to eat this Passover with you before I suffer. For I tell you, I will not eat it again until it finds fulfillment in the kingdom of God." After taking the cup, he gave thanks and said, "Take this and divide it among you. For I tell you I will not drink again of the fruit of the vine until the kingdom of God comes."

Reader 1: (*mockingly*) The people stood watching, and the rulers even sneered at him. They said, "He saved others; let him save himself if he is the Christ of God, the Chosen One." The soldiers also came up and mocked him. They offered him wine vinegar and said, "If you are the king of the Jews, save yourself." There was a written notice above him, which read: THIS IS THE KING OF THE JEWS.

114

Reader 2: (*excited*) Those who went ahead and those who followed shouted, "Hosanna!" "Blessed is he who comes in the name of the Lord!"

Reader 3: (*reflective*) And he took bread, gave thanks and broke it, and gave it to them, saying, "This is my body given for you; do this in remembrance of me."

Reader 1: (*sadly*) It was now about the sixth hour, and darkness came over the whole land until the ninth hour, for the sun stopped shining. And the curtain of the temple was torn in two.

Reader 2: (*emphatically*) "Blessed is the coming kingdom of our father David!" "Hosanna in the highest!"

Reader 3: (reflective) In the same way, after the supper he took the cup, saying, "This cup is the new covenant in my blood, which is poured out for you. . . . Jesus called out with a loud voice, "Father, into your hands I commit my spirit." When he had said this, he breathed his last.

All (*shouting*): "Blessed is he who comes in the name of the Lord!"

Reader 1: "This is my body given for you."

Reader 2: "Father, forgive them, for they do not know what they are doing."

All (*shouting*): "Hosanna in the highest!"

Reader 3: "This cup is the new covenant in my blood,"

Reader 2: "into your hands I commit my spirit."

All (*shouting*): "Hosanna!"

Reader 3: "my blood"

All (*whispered*): "Forgive them."

(*Based on Mark 11:1-10, Luke 22:7-20, and Luke 23:33-38, 44-46*)

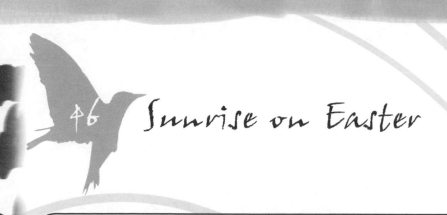

46 Sunrise on Easter

Supplies

- Empty cross, Bibles for each youth

- All songs can be found on *Iworship*.

The Experience: Wake up your youth for an early morning Easter service. Meet outside around an empty cross and have breakfast with Jesus following the service. If you literally have the service at sunrise, encourage youth to come as they are, have breakfast, and then go home to get ready for the regular Easter festivities.

Environment: early morning, sunrise; informal

Setup: Place a cross somewhere around your church yard. Gather around the cross for the service and plan to go out to breakfast following the worship time.

Senses: *Visuals*—sunrise, empty cross; *sounds*—outdoors; *smells*—freshness of morning; *touch*—the cross; *taste*—breakfast

Order of Service

Greeting: Invite a youth to greet everyone and say an opening prayer

Praising God:
        "Lord, I Lift Your Name on High"
        "Awesome God"

Scripture Reading:
        John 20:1-23 (*the Resurrection*) (*Have everyone participate in the reading and read with joy.*)

Reflection: Have a time of reflection on what the Christ's Resurrection means for the world. Encourage youth to think about ways in which they have lived as Easter people. Commit as a group to celebrate Easter year-round—not just one day a year.

Praising God:
        "That's Why We Praise Him"
        "Above All"
        "Every Move I Make"

Benediction: Invite a volunteer to pray a blessing on your group as you go to celebrate Easter with a fellowship breakfast at your favorite restaurant.

47 A Service for Pentecost

The Experience: This is an anointing service for Pentecost. Invite the Spirit to come in a powerful way into your community. Help the worshipers experience the Spirit and leave empowered to live their gifts in the world. Fill the room with bright lights and fans blowing wind throughout the worship space.

Environment: Bright room with a few candles lit; red banners; scrolling images of fire, wind, and doves; celebratory music playing

Setup: Place chairs or rugs in a semicircle around an altar table. Have the band set up to the side of the semicircle. Prepare an appropriate space for the time of anointing. Place several fans around the room and leave them on high speed throughout the service. Have two different screens if possible: one for scrolling images, one for words of music/Scriptures. Let the images scroll through the whole service. Hang bright red and white banners around the room and draped over the altar. Set a small dish of oil on the altar table.

Senses: *Visuals*—banners; *sounds*—wind from fans, music; *touch*—blowing wind, oil

Supplies

- Several fans, bright red and white fabric for banners
- Candles and matches
- Oil
- Pictures of fire, wind, and doves projected on screens
- "Madly," on *Our Love Is Loud* CD, by Passion Worship Band
- "Let It Rain," on *Worship*, by Michael W. Smith
- "Light the Fire," on *Light the Fire* CD, by Liam Lawton

Order of Service

Opening Praise and Worship: "Light the Fire"
     "Let It Rain"

Testimony: *(Invite volunteers to talk about the movement of the Spirit in their lives.)*

Scripture Reading: Acts 2:1-13 *(the day of Pentecost)*

The Message: "Living in the Spirit"

Offering: Encourage the youth to give something to the church. If they do not have money with them, encourage them to write on a piece of paper a gift of service or prayer that they intend to offer to the church.

Prayer: "God of the rushing wind and the fiery flames, we give you thanks for calling us unto yourself. Thank you for making the church where we can worship, serve, and live your love in the world. Forgive us for the time we spend tearing down the church instead of building it up and loving you more. Thank you for the gift of oil. As the apostles anointed the sick with oil, bless this oil that we might be anointed for wholeness and unity as the church. Make us one in Christ Jesus. Amen."

Anointing With Oil: *(Have the participants come forward to be anointed with oil by making the sign of the cross on their forehead. Encourage the worshipers, after they have been anointed with oil, to stand in front of a fan [not too close] as they pray in silence. Invite them to feel the rushing*

117

wind of God blowing into their lives and empowering them to be a thriving member of the church by offering their gifts to the world in the name of Jesus Christ.)

Silence

Closing Song: "Madly"

Teaching Points

- Pentecost is about power—the power of the Holy Spirit that transforms Jesus' followers and the whole world.

- What were the dynamics of Pentecost and who was involved?
    1. Individuals who had intimacy with Jesus
       __ A diverse group—women, men, doubters, deniers, and so on (verses 14-15)
       __ Can we find ourselves in that mix?

    2. Individuals who had community with other followers
       __ God loves community and creates by means of covenant throughout the Scriptures.
       __ Jesus had his band of followers.
       __ Community is about caring and serving together because of a common purpose.

    3. Individuals who influenced their world
       __ It's simply not enough to have intimacy with Jesus and community with others. Jesus calls us to make an impact on our world. We need intimacy and community with the world.
       __ The disciples went out into the streets and proclaimed the gospel (even in another language).
       __ What is the source of our ability to make an impact? The Holy Spirit, which fills us with power and strength and fills us with God.
       __ God gives us the words to say and the work to do, but we are often afraid to allow God to work through us in such a dynamic way.

    4. How is God rushing into your life and giving you a purpose for the world?
       __ How will you tell others?
       __ How will you serve the poor and needy?
       __ How will you love at all costs?
       __ How will you rely on the Holy Spirit's power to fill you and give you peace?

Pentecost Party

The Experience: Decorate the worship space as if a birthday party is in progress, with red as the dominant color. Provide a red birthday cake. Celebrate the Spirit and the birthday of the church with games, praise and worship, and *lectio divina*.

Environment: Create the feeling of a birthday party with games, balloons, and so on.

Setup: Gather everyone around a large table. Distribute red birthday hats and red party favors. Place a "Pentecost Birthday Cake" in the center of the table.

Senses: *Visuals*—party decorations; *sounds*—laughter, music, repetitive reading, silence; *touch*—games; *taste*—Pentecost Birthday Cake

Supplies

- Red decorations, red birthday cake

- Balloons

- "Light the Fire," on *Light the Fire* CD, by Liam Lawton

- "Spirit Song" and "Spirit of the Living God," found in most hymnals

Order of Service

Opening: Have one of the worshipers tap his or her glass as if getting ready to make a speech but instead she or he reads aloud Acts 2:1-4 as a greeting. Then explain to the group why we celebrate Pentecost [consider doing a bit of research about Pentecost and your faith tradition]. Talk to the participants about Pentecost being the birthday of the church, a time when the Spirit called the very first church leaders. Next, invite everyone to enjoy the Pentecost cake.

Celebration of the Spirit: (After eating, play some childhood favorite party games— pin the tail on the donkey, hopscotch, and so on.)

Praise and Worship: "Light the Fire"
"Spirit Song"
"Spirit of the Living God"

Lectio Divina Reading: Joel 2:28-29 (*God's Spirit poured out*)

Instruct the participants to close their eyes and focus on their breathing. Tell them that you are going to read a passage through three times.

1st Reading: *Say:* "As I read the passage this first time, I want you to just listen to the text. Don't try to think about it, just simply listen to it." (*Read the text aloud.*) Silence.

2nd Reading: *Say:* "As I read the passage this time, I want you to listen for a word or phrase that jumps out at you. Once you have your word or phrase in mind, simply repeat it to yourself over and over." (*Read the text again.*) Silence.

3rd Reading: *Say:* "As I read the passage one last time, I want you to imagine that the prophet is talking to you. What vision or dream do you see through this reading?" (*Read the text a third time.*) Silence.

Offering: (*Invite the worshipers to talk about ways the Scripture spoke to them. Encourage them to consider how they could be an offering to God in the church. Talk about how they will renew their commitment to God's church. Give each of the participants a red birthday candle as a symbol that God's spirit is present within them.*)

Closing Prayer: (*Invite different worshipers to lead the prayer.*)

119

Thanks for the Meal

49

Supplies

- Table decorations

- A full meal, nice dinnerware and cloth napkins, Communion elements

- A candle for each place setting

- Recorded instrumental music

- "Father, I Adore You"; "Honor and Praise"; and "O Lord, You're Beautiful," in *The Faith We Sing* (cross only edition— ISBN: 0687049040)

- "Great is Thy Faithfulness," in most hymnals

- *Conversations* CD, by Sara Groves

The Experience: This service is a celebration of Thanksgiving. In the Scripture, shared meals were formative times for community and sharing together in Christ's love. Have a meal together during this service as you also celebrate Holy Communion.

Environment: candlelit room set like a dining hall, instrumental music playing

Setup: Have chairs set around an elaborately set dining table. Set the Communion elements in the center of the table. The instrumentalist should be at one end of the table. Choose a menu and have the table set for a feast. Have a single unlit candle for each table setting.

Senses: *Visuals*—table decorations; *sounds*—music, testimonies; *smells*—food; *touch*—the Thanksgiving meal; *taste*—the meal, Communion

Order of Service

Greeting: "Welcome to our feast of Thanksgiving. We have come here to praise God for the bountiful blessings in our lives and to worship God as created beings. As we come to the banquet table of the Lord, you are invited to light the candle in front of you to unite your light with the light of Christ, to give light to the space around us, and to mark your full presence in worship this day."

Praise and Worship:
"Great Is Thy Faithfulness"
"Father, I Adore You"
"Honor and Praise"

Thanksgiving Testimonies: (*Invite all the worshipers to offer a statement of thanksgiving.*)

Praise and Worship: The Doxology

Blessing and Sharing of God's Goodness: (*Give thanks for the meal and feast together. As the participants begin to finish their meal, move into the next part of the service. [People can still be eating as the Scripture is read.]*)

Scripture Reading: Lamentations 3:19-30 (*God is faithful.*)

Worship Song: (*If possible, have someone sing "He's Always Been Faithful," by Sara Groves. If this song is not available to you, have someone sing a song of thanksgiving.*)

The Message: "Thanks for the Meal"

120

Holy Communion: (*Celebrate Communion by passing around the table a loaf of bread and a cup of juice in which to dip the bread.*)

Silence and Prayer: (*Allow ten minutes of silence for the community to reflect on the message or simply give thanks to God. Play some background music.*)

Praise and Worship: "O Lord, You're Beautiful"

Benediction: (*Have the worshipers stand and hold hands.*) "Thanks be to God for the nourishment of food, community, faith, and love. May we never forget to call to mind the faithfulness of God at all times. Amen."

Teaching Points

- Recall the text: The author of the Scripture is writing from a place of immense pain. Read the previous verses leading up to our lesson. The writer endured fierce pain and affliction; but even in suffering, the writer "called to mind" the faithfulness of God.

- Consider the history of Thanksgiving. Harsh winters, wars, failed crops—these conditions led a group of people to give thanks when they called goodness to mind.

- To serve Christ is to surrender to the One whom we allow to live through us. In hard times, when things happen that we don't understand, in beauty and bounty, Christ lives in us and we call to mind the steadfast love of God.

- Tonight, this same Jesus invites us to a meal to feast and to drink deeply of his love. He loves us and is willing to be with us even though we struggle to surrender to him. The Lord is good. Wait quietly for the Lord.

Supplies

- Symbols, images, and colored fabric for each season
- Potluck meal
- Hymnals

The Experience: Many youth and adults have little understanding of the cycle of the Christian year. Some grew up in churches that don't pay much attention to traditional liturgical seasons. Persons who are new to the faith may not have learned about these patterns in Sunday school or confirmation classes. This service will give the participants a chance to relive the entire church year in about an hour, as well as understand the many connections each season has to the patterns of their life.

Environment: Create a feeling of festival and celebration in the worship space.

Setup: Make a slide for each season with its name, liturgical colors, and a symbol. Collect images, videos, symbols, and props appropriate to each liturgical season, such as these suggested items:

Advent
Images of Mary and John the Baptist; waiting (waiting for a taxi, standing in line, being pregnant, and so on); advent wreath
Color: Dark blue/purple (*A banner, sheet, or long strip of fabric can be used if your church does not have altar cloths.*)

Christmas
Images of the birth of Jesus, angels, Christmas tree, Nativity sets
Color: White

Epiphany
Images of the magi, gifts, baptism
Color: Gold

Lent
Images of the Last Supper, the garden of Gethsemane, Jesus being tried and crucified, ashes, palm branches, Communion elements
Color: Purple

Easter
Images of the Resurrection, women going to the tomb, empty tombs, grave clothes, empty cross, early morning light
Color: White and gold

Pentecost/Kingdomtide
Images of doves, flames, and candles
Color: Various colors (incorporating red, white, and green)

Set up the room so that the seasons are represented in order and in different parts of the room. If the chairs can be moved, consider physically moving everyone from place to place with each season. Or sit around round tables with items representing each season on each table. Feel free to use other hymns or songs that your group will know well that fit the themes of each season. You may also use recorded songs if you prefer. Select several readers and assign a season to each. One person should ask the questions throughout the service. Project the questions if you have proper equipment. After the service share a meal together with different foods that represent different times of the year. Assign a holiday to each youth and have them bring a dish that they connect to their season.

Senses: *Visuals*—symbols for each season; *sounds*—music for different seasons; *touch*—moving to each seasons' station; *taste*—buffet after service

Order of Service

Prelude: (*Play a variety of recorded songs representing each liturgical season, or have the band play appropriate hymns and songs for different times in the church year.*)

Greeting: "Today you will experience an entire Christian year in about an hour. Just as certain things happen every year at the same time—birthdays, holidays, school events, and so on—the church year has patterns and cycles. We call these cycles the liturgical year, a year that is made up of seven seasons. We will journey through the church year and briefly experience a little bit of each season. So let's get started!"

Introduction (*new reader*): "The writer of the Book of Ecclesiastes reminds us that "for everything there is a season and a time for every matter under heaven" (3:1). The seasons of the church year—Advent, Christmas, Epiphany, Lent, Easter, Pentecost, and the Season after Pentecost—form a framework for following the life of Jesus. As we go through the year, we experience all the major events of his life. We follow Jesus' life so that the life of Jesus might live in us. Celebrating these seasons shapes us to be more like Jesus. As we explore each season, you will have a chance to talk about your memories of seasons past and how each season relates to your spiritual journey."

Advent

Scripture: Matthew 3:1-12 (*Have someone memorize this passage before the service and then read it in costume.*)

Song: "O Come, O Come, Emmanuel" or "Come, Thou Long-Expected Jesus"

Reading: "At the beginning of the Christian year, we wait. In the four weeks of Advent, we are waiting for the coming of Christ—the first coming of Jesus as the baby in Bethlehem, and the second coming of Jesus to complete the transformation of the world. We wait; and during our waiting, we prepare ourselves to give birth. One medieval man proclaimed that we are all intended to be mothers of God, to give birth to the holy. He wrote, "Become aware of what is in you. Announce it, pronounce it, produce it, and give birth to it" (Meister Eckhart). Like Mary, we are called to respond to the Spirit of God with an offering of who we are and what we have: "Let it be with me according to your word.""

Discussion

- What are your favorite memories of Advent from when you were younger?
- What things are hardest to wait for in your spiritual life?
- What does it mean to you to give birth to the holy?

Christmas

Scripture: Matthew 1:18-25

Song: "Joy to the World"

Reading: "The tree is lit; candles are burning; the sanctuary is dark and warm. Around you people are singing "Silent Night." As you celebrate the birth of Jesus, you find that your skin tingles with awareness; your grandma's eyes brim with tears. You are filled with gratitude and awe. Our God is made known through flesh—a mystery that fills us with a speechless wonder. 'Wonder,' wrote Thomas Carlyle, 'is the basis of worship' (*Sartor Resartus*). The lesson of the Christmas season expands far beyond late December and early January. We are to cultivate a way of looking at the world that allows us to see God in everything—the birth of a baby, the stars in the sky, the lowing of cattle, the family on our street. Worship happens when we are in touch with the majesty of creation, the gift our lives, and the love of our God."

Discussion

- What are the most meaningful parts of the Christmas season for you?
- When have you experienced wonder in your life of faith?
- What does it mean to you that God came to earth as we do, not great and powerful, but as a tiny, frail child?

Epiphany

Scripture: Matthew 2:1-12

Song: "We Three Kings"

Reading: "The life of faith is filled with choices. One of these is the choice of how to respond to Jesus—with faith like the magi, or with fear like King Herod. To have faith is to trust, to commit to something greater than ourselves, to believe in something that to many sounds downright ridiculous. Faith is active, moving us forward to something new. Fear, on the other hand, keeps us from moving. It paralyzes and controls us, makes us lash out at the unknown, and makes us avoid potential threats, both real and imagined. During Epiphany, when all the decorations are put away and the vacation is over, we are asked to make a choice that will affect everything that follows. Will we embrace the Christ Child, God's Son, with faith; or will we shrink away in fear?"

Discussion

- Describe a time in your life when you were faced with making a choice between faith and fear.
- What new action has faith moved you toward recently?

Lent

Scripture: Joel 2:1-2, 12-16

Song: "Were You There"

Reading: "We are only able to keep love when we are in the habit of loving others. During Lent, we journey with Jesus as he gives away his love. For forty days, we immerse ourselves in the stories of the self-giving, sacrificial love of Jesus. During Holy Week, we enter Jerusalem and watch as Jesus' love is betrayed, beaten, crucified. All along the way, we examine our own hearts and confess the selfishness and sin lodged deep within us. From Ash Wednesday, when we take burnt ashes of palms and symbolically remember our mortality through the sign of the cross on our forehead, through Good Friday, the day Jesus was executed, our Lenten prayer is simple: 'Teach us to love.' "

Discussion

- How is the love that Jesus demonstrates and calls us to, different from the love we see and hear about in popular culture?
- Which is more significant for you—the life of Jesus or his death? Why?

Easter

Scripture: Mark 16:1-14

Song: "Hymn of Promise"

Reading: For fifty days from Easter Sunday through the Day of Pentecost, we remind ourselves that we are a people of song and dance, a people of feasting and celebration. With the great fifty days of the Easter season, we proclaim that death was not the end for Jesus, and that death is not the end for us. We are not left alone or abandoned. The Holy Spirit is with us. Our tears are transformed into laughter, our heartache into brilliant hope. Jesus says to us, 'These things have I spoken to you, that my joy may be in you, and that your joy may be full.' With the rising of the sun, the trumpeting of lilies, the singing of Alleluias, we join with all of creation in praising God. In the Easter season, we listen carefully to our lives and to the world and we hear that life is not just suffering and sadness. We hear instead the miraculous assurance that the heartbeat of the world is God's joy.

Discussion

- What does it mean to live as "Easter people," as people changed by the Resurrection?
- Jesus is alive! How is he alive in you and in the world today?

Pentecost

Scripture: Acts 2:1-17

Songs: "Spirit of the Living God"
                                        "Sanctuary"

Reading: "As one poet has put it, 'The winds of grace are always blowing. You have only to raise your sail' (*Ramakrishna*). After the day of Pentecost when the disciples felt the Holy Spirit come as a wind from heaven and as tongues of fire resting on their heads, the work of the church began. In the Christian calendar, the season after Pentecost is the longest of all, lasting almost half of the year. Sometimes we call this season "ordinary time" as if the days pass with little to report. And yet, this is the season when we are called to live a passionate life, a life of faith that has been set on fire. This is a season when we are called to be co-creators with God, to lift our sails and be propelled by the winds of the Spirit. This is a season when we are to be passionately engaged in a life of love and service. It's the season when we're all reminded that we're charged by Jesus with a mission and a purpose—to tell the world of God's love, and to make disciples of all nations."

Discussion
- What are the things that cause your faith to be passionate and alive? What things tend to quench that fire?
- What does it mean to be a co-creator with God in the daily activities of your life?

Song: "Spirit of the Living God"

The Year at a Glance: "Our Christian year helps us remember the story of Jesus. By living through the liturgical year, we participate in the birth, life, death, and resurrection of our Lord. How will you live your faith story this year?" (*Open a discussion with the youth of learnings, questions, and challenges to participating in the Christian story through the year.*)

Benediction: "For everything there is a season and a purpose for every matter under heaven. Every so often when you look at your calendar, think to yourself, *What season is this?* and remind yourself of the things we remember about Jesus' life during that season. But most important, whatever season it is, remember that all time is God's time and that every day is a new opportunity for serving Jesus. Amen."

Feast: Gather around the banquet table and feast on food and fellowship!

Suggested Resources for Postmodern Worship

Multimedia Resources

Iworship: A Total Worship Experience

This is an amazing worship tool for multisensory worship. A two-disc CD contains 33 popular worship songs. Complete song tracks and a CD-ROM enhanced songbook are available as well as a DVD component with lyrics set on beautiful images. iworship is a total multimedia worship experience that combines the latest advances in audiovisual presentations with the most powerful songs in the church today. The multimedia resource combines powerful worship songs with audiovisual presentations to make your worship a holy experience. To purchase visit *iworshipnow.com*.

The Faith We Sing (Pew Edition, Cross Only Cover) (ISBN: 0687049040)

This songbook is ecumenical songbook rich in global praise music, new hymns, Taizé and Iona chants, and popular praise songs. Nowhere else will you find the rich combination of music in one resource. Complete with a guitar edition, MIDI edition, presentation edition, and a CD-ROM edition. *The Faith We Sing* is a must have! Buy it at *TheFaithWeSing.com*.

Verticallife: A Youth Ministry Worship Resource (Version 2.1)

Verticallife is a subscription service. Each issue includes a demonstration CD with 10 popular modern worship songs, accompaniment tracks on CD, PowerPoint® compatible lyrics, transparency masters with lyrics, chord charts and rhythm charts, and MediaShout® media—for ministry presentation software. This resource will keep you up to date with the latest worship music and equip you, your leaders, and musicians. Learn more about the resource and subscribe at *verticallife.com*.

Songbooks

Songs for Taizé (ISBN: 2850401285)

For a deeper prayer and meditative experience in worship, familiarize yourself with the tradition of Taizé prayer services. The songs are sung repetitively so as to begin to live and breathe the prayers. Learn more about Taizé at *www.taizé.fr*.

Passion Songbook (ISBN: 3474012967)

This new compilation songbook features every song recorded on all four Passion projects. It contains sheet music for the piano and guitar, chord sheets for guitar, and overhead masters for congregational/Bible study use.

Compact Discs

David Crowder Band—*Can You Hear Us?*

Charlie Hall—*Porch and Altar*

Passion Worship Band—*OneDay Live*

Passion Worship Band—*The Road to OneDay*

Passion Worship Band—*Our Love Is Loud: Live*

Passion Worship Band—*Better Is OneDay*

Passion Worship Band—*Passion '98: Live Worship From the 268 Generation: Live*

Michael W. Smith—*Worship*

Chris Tomlin—*Not to Us*

Chris Tomlin—*The Noise We Make*

Cathedral of Sound: Global DJ Experience

Websites

worshiptogether.com
This website will keep you current on the worship scene with the latest songs from today's most popular worship leaders and songs. Buy CDs, songbooks, chordcharts, and more.

arttoheartweb.com/worship_resources.htm
Learn how to use classical paintings in worship, and find out more about worship styles and resources.

www.sacramentis.com
Look for poetry, graphics, and articles about postmodern worship.

www.theooze.com
Find a listing of links to churches in your state meeting the worshiping needs of postmodern youth.

www.emergentvillage.com
Join a community of church leaders who are studying and anticipating cultural shifts and how those shifts play out in the church.